salty

salty

THE DECONSTRUCTION OF A GOOD CHRISTIAN

HOLLYLU JOSTES

REDEMPTION PRESS

Published by Redemption Press, PO Box 427, Enumclaw, WA 98022.
Toll-Free (844) 2REDEEM (273-3336)

ISBN 13: 978-1-64645-605-5 (Paperback)
978-1-64645-604-8 (ePub)
978-1-64645-603-1 (Mobi)

Library of Congress Catalog Card Number: 2022903932

Dedication

DEDICATED TO MY PARENTS: FOR DAD WHO TAUGHT ME TO seek adventure and that life is mostly what you make it—so make it sunshine. And Mom who taught me to stay at the feet of the Master, regardless of circumstance. A promise made is a promise kept.

Also dedicated to my husband, Michael. Thank you for taking the adventure with me and for being a leader I want to follow. Also thank you for understanding that coffee is medicinal and for keeping me out of jail. All of my love—but more specifically, all of my respect. Forever and always.

Finally—dedicated to Anna and Teddy. Because of you, I understand the love of God so much better. Faith is not blind. God's call is not opposed to our intellect, but not limited by it either.

Contents

Acknowledgements

I WHOLEHEARTEDLY ACKNOWLEDGE THE AMAZING PASTORS who labored so diligently to illuminate my dim bulb. Despite being imperfect themselves, they clearly pointed to a perfect Father, and I am forever indebted. Also, a blanket apology for the wax all over the sanctuary stairs and for the live chicken loose in the church. I neither confirm nor deny involvement as I have not matured beyond culpability.

I also thank the big brains for explaining gigantic truth in stepping stones I could follow: Dallas Willard, Carolyn Custis James, John Ortberg, Timothy Keller, C. S. Lewis, A. W. Tozer, D. L. Moody, Oswald Chambers, G. K. Chesterton, Jonathan Edwards, Hannah Whitehall Smith, and so many more. Although I argued with you, scribbled and marked up your pages, and slammed your writings on many hard surfaces—you always forgave me, and we started again. Now that's grace.

I want to deeply acknowledge the tribe of Ezers who did the hardest work of all—being present and active in my life across the decades. To be a friend is complicated. To stay a friend is courageous. In the friend department, I have been blessed with an embarrassment of riches, too many dear women to list. However, I do want to thank Jodi, Beth, Dana, and Melissa for pulling and pushing alongside me to finish this God-given task. Because of you, I didn't quit.

Finally, an enormous thank you to Sara and the staff at Redemption Press for persisting with the most reluctant, distracted, champion-level procrastinator to ever pick up a pen. Your professionalism and care is life sustaining. Keep up His good work.

CHAPTER 1

The Death of a Good Christian

Once conform, once do what other people do because they do it, and a lethargy steals over all the finer nerves and faculties of the soul. She becomes all outer show and inward emptiness; dull, callous, and indifferent.

—Virginia Woolf, "Montaigne," in *The Common Reader*

ONE MORNING, I WAS LATE TO HUDDLE. HUDDLE IS CODE FOR *no chairs allowed*. I'm not sure what chairs did to get themselves banned from hospital staff meetings, but ten people squished into a space designed to accommodate six is not a groovy way to start the day.

Clinging to my coffee mug, I stood in the back, looking at the floor. Making eye contact isn't recommended when you're late to huddle. Late people either have some urgent news to share with the group, or they are in need of some gentle public shaming. I had no news and needed no shame. I brought my own with me. A new friend—a physician—arrived behind me. Doctors have different timelines. He was safe from ridicule—at least the public kind.

He bumped my bag sliding into the room. Did I mention there are *no* chairs and too many people? We ended up squished shoulder to shoulder. Apologizing, he noticed my mug. Bright pink and covered in daisies, it featured a boldly printed Bible verse about strength.

"Sweet," he whispered, pointing to the cheery flowers. "I can always spot you Christians. You have the nicest coffee cups."

I looked up into his eyes. He smiled. My new friend was from the Middle East. He was a good physician and happened to be Muslim.

As religious people, we were often on the same side of philosophical lunchtime banter. I looked down at my mug. And somewhere deep inside, the lights flickered.

I needed air. "I have to go," I whispered, slithering out of the clump of bodies.

I stumbled back to my office to shed my clipboard and treatment bag. But the coffee mug stayed with me.

Taking the elevator to the ground floor, I walked out into the misty Northwest morning. Always wet, rarely raining. The parked cars were wedged together, forcing me to weave back and forth in order to cross the lot. I headed toward a pitiful square of grass reserved for those who smoke. Much dejection and misery are heaped upon healthcare workers addicted to nicotine. Polluting one's body in an institution designed to fix polluted bodies is scandalous.

The forlorn little patch was located exactly fifty yards from the hospital door. It was vacant. Not even junkies needed a fix this early in the shift. Overwhelmingly fatigued, I balanced myself on a section of broken curb. Chairs were banned from these meetings too.

What was I doing here? Why was I suddenly so upset? My mind was racing and vacant at the same time. My gaze settled on my coffee mug, and I read its verse aloud: "The joy of the Lord is my strength." I couldn't remember the last time I had felt the Lord's joy. Or any kind of joy, for that matter. I read the verse a few more times, and the lights flickered again.

I nestled the mug amid the discarded cigarette butts on the ground and reached for a small chunk of concrete. Raising my arm up into the sky, I brought the chunk down, sending shards of pink and white into the gray and green.

Startled by my own behavior, I sat back on my haunches and studied the mess. It was a pretty good job. I couldn't read the verse anymore.

Why did that feel satisfying?

Rebellion scratches an itch. It satiates, at least temporarily, the ache of living with too many truths. Much of my faith made no sense at all. So many Bible verses—the claims of Christianity—felt hollow.

What *exactly* was "the joy of the Lord," and why did I never feel it? If I never actually felt what the verses claimed God would deliver, then what was all the work, all the worry, and all the overwhelming guilt for?

For the first time, I didn't know what I believed. And while stooping there in the squalor of addiction, I realized that I hadn't known for quite some time. How ironic. In this place designed to publicly disapprove of what is legally tolerated, I felt nothing but disdain for my own dualistic existence. I was a poster child for Jesus, yet unsure why Jesus never lived up to his billing.

If I no longer knew what I believed, then I would no longer carry on as if I did. If I couldn't live by the words on the mug, I would refuse to carry it.

It was a moment that deserved a lot more time to think. But my feet were getting cold. Existential breakdowns are not convenient, and I needed to get back to the business of the day. I stooped and began collecting the pieces. One shard had landed a full four feet away. It had been a powerful blow.

Joy might come from the Lord. But apparently, strength can come from all kinds of places.

I'm not the first Christ-follower to go rogue, although smashing a coffee mug was pretty original. Looking back, the rawness of the moment still stings. I also wonder why my little melodrama was going down in the smoker's patch.

Because I've never smoked. But I do go to church, three blessed times a week.

Hmm.

If we polled all the people currently sitting in the pew, my guess is that they'd unanimously endorse attending church. Going to church is good, right? But if the poll was anonymous, and we asked the same people if they felt safe having a meltdown in same said pew, I think the answer would be an overwhelming *no*. Because church is not a very safe place. A good place, perhaps. But safe? No.

Why?

Because fake happens.

The modern Western church knows a lot about fake, and I do too. Fake goes like this: I love God. He's good, and he's powerful, and I want to be on his team. But I don't want to work or suffer or face hardship. Because doesn't God want me to be happy? Of course he does. So I'm going to wear the jersey. I just don't want to sweat or anything. *Eww.*

And in order to avoid sweating, I avoid trying to understand all that stuff in the Bible. The contract, the playbook, the team archives. My goal—if I were focused enough to actually form one—would be to join Team God, then spend my time standing around on the side of the field. Maybe volunteer to bring snacks or something. Then I'd be covered. And I wouldn't smell like sweat.

Granted, the modern Western church's experience with this isn't unique. Christ-followers have been guilty of the whole fake thing since we stumbled out of the garden. There's lots of data on it. It's called the Old Testament. Claiming to believe something and then acting contrary to that belief. This is the story of Adam and Eve. And the Israelites in the desert. And the judges and kings. It's our corporate story. Lots of professing belief, but little acting on that belief.

Welcome to church, 'Merica. At least, our overwhelming version of it.

Perhaps this sounds harsh. Admittedly, I am culpable. Paul considered himself to be the chief of all sinners, but really? Pipe down, your Apostleship. The internet didn't even exist yet.

Nope. Here in the modern Western world, we deal with something tougher. We have illusion. The illusion of power, strength, control. All of this illusion clouds what's really going on. Elsewhere in the world, folks who spend fourteen hours a day attempting to feed their families have an advantage. Clarity.

It's a gift to glimpse the world as it truly is. Broken. Fallen. Dead. When we're aware of the dark, the light is so much easier to see. We should have compassion for comfortable people. For wealthy and talented people. For people with perfectly defined abs or thousands of followers on social media. Blinded by illusion, we head off to church believing in God but unwilling to commit to a life of discipleship.

After all, the football playoffs start at noon, right? Plus, there's the pregame coverage.

And so the walls of many churches bulge with completely well-intentioned fake people. With untested commitment and unpracticed conviction, we wear team jerseys with Jesus's name on the back. And we live with one foot on God's field and one foot on our own field until the illusion is shattered.

The problem with illusions is that they're designed to look and feel real.

> To the angel of the church in Laodicea write: These are the words of the Amen, the faithful and true witness, the ruler of God's creation. I know your deeds, that you are neither cold nor hot. I wish you were either one or the other! So, because you are lukewarm—neither hot nor cold—I am about to spit you out of my mouth. (Revelation 3:14–16)

It's worth asking if *lukewarm* is synonymous with *fake*. Fake somehow feels insulting. I've heard this statement in my Bible study circle: "I might be a little lukewarm, but I don't think I'm fake." That's laughable. Are we trying to manage the terms that describe our lameness? Sort of like, "That dress makes you look less fat."

The connection between lukewarm and fake is pretty clear. But heaven forbid we use logic in church. At some point, I basically volunteered to stop thinking. Perhaps more precisely, I allowed distraction to keep me from thinking too deeply.

Because living a double standard is a logical sticky wicket, and the maintenance bill is steep.

I know this personally. My evolution into a full-blown Good Christian is the perfect illustration of this relationship between lukewarm and fake.

I accepted Jesus as my personal Savior at the tender age of four. My mother simply explained the offer of salvation, a free gift from a God who loved me. I either believed it or I didn't. And I was no fool.

I believed.

In my stalwart Midwest family, we went to church three times a week. But the same intelligence that drove me to accept God's offer also drove me to question what I learned. I actually listened in Sunday school, and the stuff being taught was rather disturbing.

Kids who grow up in church hear the stories in the gospel accounts many, many times. And the first dozen times or so, I had some serious concerns. John the Baptist, the cousin of Jesus, was beheaded. The apostle Paul was beaten, flogged, shipwrecked, and imprisoned. James, one of Jesus's closest friends, was run clear through with a sword. The list of pain and problems faced by Christians, most often as a result of their faith, was long. Looking into the caring, wrinkled faces of my Sunday school teachers, I wondered, "Do you people hear what you're saying?"

When I did raise questions, I was taught the right answers. The world won't accept Christ-followers any more than it accepted Jesus. Our faith will sustain us in times of trouble. Those committed to Christ ultimately find the suffering small in comparison to the joy found in following him.

And to encourage us, church leaders told harrowing stories of great missionaries of the faith. And by harrowing, I mean every single one dies. Usually of dysentery. Always dressed in unfashionable clothes.

Consider Hudson Taylor. One bright week of my childhood summers, his story was spread across five days of vacation Bible school. Hudson, one of the first missionaries to China, founded the China Inland Mission. Arguably the first Anglo missionary to work within—not against—native culture, Hudson shed his prudish Victorian clothing for the Chinese long shirt and wore his hair braided in a thick tail down his back. I remember listening intently to Hudson's story because, unlike the flannelgraph Bible lesson before it, I hadn't heard this story a million times. This man was a rebel, a crusader, an activist, and above all, a humble servant to his God. And he had my attention.

His life's story highlights are as follows: On Monday, Hudson taught himself to sleep on a plank of wood so that he would be prepared for the life of a missionary. On Tuesday, he left for China and survived two typhoons. On Wednesday, the people whom Hudson came to serve rioted in the streets, burning his house and church to the ground. Shortly after the riot, his daughter died of sickness. On Thursday, two more children died, followed by his beloved wife, Maria. Then Hudson was nearly paralyzed falling off a riverboat.

At this point, we were pretty horrified. We didn't know if we should root for Hudson or encourage him to cash it in. On Friday, his second wife died, two more children died, and finally Hudson himself died alone in Changsha, China, hundreds of miles from his nearest relatives.

The man was personally responsible for recruiting over 800 missionaries to his beloved adopted country. Although Hudson was a stranger to me, I recognized the gospel story inside his life. A crazy, full-bore allegiance to God. A drive, a willingness to surrender, and an insistence that following God wasn't a promise of pain-free living. Conversely, it appeared to be a complete shunning of the glamorous while embracing a life of toil and sweat. A lot of sweat.

At the conclusion of Friday's lesson, our Bible teacher paused and took a deep breath. With a rapturous look upon her lightly powdered face, she proclaimed, "Our prayer for each of you children is that you would grow up to serve God just like Hudson Taylor."

Umm.

I loved Jesus. But I didn't want to sleep on a board. I didn't want to be shipwrecked and beaten up, and I really didn't want to go to China. I wanted to go to Claire's and buy earrings *made in China*. Thank you.

I wondered if there might be a plan B. Like, could I believe in Jesus but not sign up for trouble? Could I work on keeping myself safe and check in with God on the weekends? Granted, I was a kid, and these thoughts were muddled up by the fuzziness of a developing mind. But there was a conscious effort there. How could I follow God *and* be safe, warm, and happy—and possibly, good looking, popular, and wealthy?

And that marked the beginning of my transition to a Good Christian. My desire was to be in the club but not a Gold Star member. It was basically a control thing. I wanted assurance that would keep me out of hell, but I didn't want to relinquish control over my mind or heart. And sweet mother of pearl, no one better put a hand on my wallet.

In my mind I approached a crossroads. I would either reject this faith, or I would stop thinking too deeply. The third option of total commitment wasn't even on my radar. The Bible calls for radical behavior. It demands movement, and it probes and challenges. On some level, it's clear even to children—God wants everything. Every part of life. He wants the dreams, the desires, the talent. He wants the deep, broken places. All of it. There is no tithing of self.

Tithing of self? Yes. Tithing is a term used by Christians. It refers to the discipline of giving one's resources to the ongoing work of God. As a kid, I was taught all about tithing. Good Christians tithe 10 percent of their income. So I gave 10 percent of my babysitting earnings and also 10 percent—roughly speaking—of me. This worked out to about $1.75 and four hours a week.

You're welcome, God.

Did I actually do the math? Well, no. But I taught myself to help at church on Sundays. I gave my best effort helping with little kids, singing, praying, and serving coffee. And then I left the church building and lived my life. I didn't want pain or suffering, especially not as result of my faith. Life presented enough challenges without inviting trouble.

At this point, a question often emerges. Are Good Christians actually saved? You can read all the theology books and debate the point in countless blogs—while young people and people with limited attention spans grow ever more disenchanted with organized religion—but I can answer only for myself. Yes, I was saved. I believe with all of my soul that if I'd been taken out by a truck while illegally crossing the street to get to Starbucks before the line got any longer, I would've been instantly embraced by my Savior.

To make the assumption that my lackluster performance as a Christ-follower affected the status of my salvation is just too big a leap. If our behavior makes us *more* saved or somehow maintains our status as saved, then Christ's ultimate sacrifice wasn't all that ultimate. In other words, if you plant an acorn, an oak tree will grow. There might be rocks around the sprout, and it may be poorly watered and fertilized, and it may end up being a warped, mangy little oak tree. But it's still an oak tree.

While it's not hard to define how to *become* a Christian, it's certainly difficult to describe how to *live* like one. To be a disciple, one must behave like the Master Teacher. We're all basically well intentioned, and we attempt to teach and be taught by each other, but we've sort of jumbled the order. A disciple behaves like the Master Teacher because she has learned to think like the Master Teacher. A disciple is so devoted and entrenched that her brain gradually morphs until there's no other pathway as strong. There's only one way to think. One way to act. The default setting has become the way of the Master Teacher. That's how it's set up. "Be transformed by the renewing of your mind" (Romans 12:2) beautifully describes how God has designed habit to flow from thought.

But it's not easy to put that in a flannelgraph lesson. And it's much easier to see and measure and judge *behavior*. Right? It's not hard to identify sin in children. Spitting on your sister is just so obvious. So we point out *good* and *bad* to children by labeling what they do. Meaning, how they behave. As a kid, I was rewarded for saying and doing the right thing. This is Normal Church Behavior 101.

However, I was confused on how to *think* like the Master Teacher.

There were probably many saints trying to teach me this difference between outer obedience and inner surrender, but at the time I was more concerned with finding my Dr Pepper Lip Smacker that had fallen through the hole in my coat pocket. Between my poor attention span and my intense desire to remain in control of my life, it was just so much easier to outwardly act the part of the Good Christian while not bothering my inner self all that much. A follower with the caveat of only going halfway.

A subtle shift with monstrous ramifications.

Because I accepted my incomplete faith, I believed I would never be fully acceptable to God. I was the black sheep of the family. Still in the flock, just living as a disappointment to the Shepherd. The experience of God's power—and also his joy and acceptance—was out of reach. Just like my goal to be an Olympic figure skater. I might dream of gold, but it wasn't going to happen.

I always loved God. I belonged to him. I even wanted him, just not at the cost of *all* of me. And I felt a little crummy about that, but it was a tolerable amount of crummy.

Then I noticed something. When I was taking care of others, I felt a little less gross. I felt a measure of his grace and saw the working of his love. Gradually, I found a way to live as the black sheep. Working, caring, and giving became a temporary salve for the indescribable duality deep inside.

This was my action plan—work hard without surrender. It took a lot of energy to serve God while not surrendering to him. And everyone could see my faults. So instead of constantly focusing on my weaknesses and my failure as a follower, I shifted to playing up my strengths. I mean, I'm not all bad, right? Look at all the good stuff I'm doing. Phew! That feels better. Maybe it's a little fake but certainly preferable to constant burnout and discouragement. And now I was sliding on one slippery slope.

I decided to follow God, but technically only if he was going in the general direction I wanted to go. Before long, I had an "I'm fine" face—the trademark of a Good Christian—just as artificial as the pearls around my neck. Faithfully listening while not actually absorbing my weekly dose of Christianity.

Occasionally I'd wonder how I ended up sitting in this pew.

I'm pretty sure I'm not the only one who grew up like this or thought like this or felt like this. Because the fake-ification process happens on a rather subconscious level, Good Christians aren't too comfortable with people showing their brokenness outwardly. At least, not the regular attenders. The newbies are allowed some room to be messed up, but if they really want to connect and serve, they better tuck that crazy in. Brokenness is a little too genuine. It sets off a lot of internal alarms. Church is about the team we've identified with. It's not about the individual. If the goal is to live in unity, we'd better not be too different. As a congregation, we sort of band together and subconsciously—or not—repel those we perceive as weaker. Everyone does and says the right things, of course. But church can become a dangerous place for anyone not playing the game.

And it can be very, very lonely.

By now, I've either offended you or linked arms with you. This is a short summary of Good Christian Life as I experienced it—that is, living with an underdeveloped understanding of discipleship. But let me assure you that I'm not anti–Good Christian. As a person in a gradual state of recovery from this, I have huge empathy for my former tribe. Like any prisoner, Good Christians are vastly unaware of their condition. The church has built many solid programs and ministries on the backs of perpetually exhausted women who mistake fatigue for holiness. Because let's face it—Good Christians get the job done. The only way one can appear hypocritical is to embrace a standard. But to embrace God's standard without embracing God himself? Well, that's just sad. And it's a painful way to live. No wonder we become plastic.

This is my story. And it's really not that special. I hear similar versions all the time. Loving and believing in God, yet not wanting to give ourselves entirely to him. It's like being invited to a dance and accepting the invitation, then standing by the wall the entire evening. Are you at the dance? Yes. Are you having any fun at all? No. In fact, people who attend dances but don't dance are usually miserable.

This analogy sums up the Sunday morning experience for an overwhelming majority of faithful attenders. People who sit in church without surrendering to the supernatural grace, love, and mercy offered by a living God are the very definition of miserable. And to avoid misery, we distract ourselves with busyness.

Busy, miserable people.

I was mostly okay with the general direction of things. But deep inside, I knew there was a commitment that wasn't being honored. The discrepancy in the books grew wider, and then one day a choice had to be made—to die or live.

My day of reckoning came in a workplace huddle with really good people doing really good things. In that moment, I discovered the primary identification for my status as Christ-follower was a brightly colored mug. Was there anything that made me different from anyone else in that room? Besides that mug?

The answer was no.

I didn't feel different from anyone else. I knew the God of the universe, but I was frightened, worried, stressed, and angry much of the time. Standing in huddle, my pulse pounded. Like Pinocchio glimpsing himself in the mirror the moment he fully turned to wood, I felt my faith dying. Doubt clutched and squeezed my soul. My fakeness had reached critical mass.

To continue on this path, something had to die. Either my intellect or my belief.

I hadn't realized that across the parking lot by the dumpster, covered with cigarette butts and litter, was a patch of holy ground. A place where the Immortal bent down and touched the human clay. But the clay—being clay—was unaware.

Everyone has a moment. It's true that life is a series of decisions, but there is always a final choice. A place where we can fully turn away and watch the ashes of faith fall into oblivion. Or *hesitate*. And in that millisecond—inside that tiny, insignificant fragment in the enormous rolling of time—God lives. But he's not the God I thought I knew.

Standing over the broken pieces and surrounded by my ugly reality, I hesitated, not wanting to let faith die. But also not wanting to live with so many unanswered questions.

Looking back, I see more clearly. One life ended and another life began as I kneeled on the ground. How can we know which moment will change the course of everything?

People sometimes ask me, "When did you accept Christ?" It's hard to answer. Many times. Daily, I suppose. But this day I made a cataclysmic decision that shattered my illusions. It was the best and worst day of my life.

Until I stopped carrying around my coffee cup of fake, there was no running to Jesus. The Prodigal Son and the older brother have much more in common than I ever knew. It's not about the behavior—being good or being bad; it's about the Father. It's about running in his direction. From the vantage point of the older son, this is a lot harder to grasp. The older son stands there with his Starbucks and clipboard, monstrously put out by this ridiculous spectacle of grace.

This book is the story of the older son, or rather, the older daughter. The girl trying to make appropriate and God-honoring choices. The woman who tried to publicly live up to the impossible standards in Proverbs 31.

Turns out, the Good Christian was wrong. And until she died, there was no living. Until I smashed the mug, I couldn't run. And let me tell you, sister, running is where the power is found. Inside his strength, we are consumed by heaven.

And then—only then—there is joy.

CHAPTER 2

Brain-Eating Amoebas

Suppose our failures occur, not in spite of what we are doing, but precisely because of it.

—Dallas Willard, *The Divine Conspiracy: Rediscovering Our Hidden Life in God*

GOOD CHRISTIAN. THE TERM CONJURES STEREOTYPICAL NORMS regarding approved behavior. In many circles, Good Christian is simply a shorthand term used to rapidly identify people doing the right things—or conversely, to identify sinners doing wrong things. For instance, when recommending a friend who happens to be a plumber: "Oh, you should try him. He's a Good Christian."

The Good Christian label is viewed from wildly different angles inside or outside the church. The world at large tends to clump all Christians together. Hypocritical hucksters, fraudulent evangelists, and hateful militants are thrown in with the rest of us. Because of this bellwether form of notoriety, the world squints at anyone who identifies as Christian. At best, they approach suspiciously. At worst, they glare with derision.

But inside the walls of Christendom, the term Good Christian is more nuanced. It captures the working bee. The one who loves Jesus and wants to serve him. The one attempting Christlike behaviors from a deep desire to please God. And because they work hard, Good Christians carry the weight of the Western church.

Let's consider a few examples.

The Good Christian watches children before school so a single mother can get to work on time. She serves soup and hands out blankets after the hurricane. She drives an elderly neighbor to the doctor's office and takes dinner to coworkers facing sudden tragedy. She stands up to bullies and helps the weak. It's the Good Christian who covers the front desk so the secretary can take a personal call. The Good Christian cares.

Good Christians run most of the programs educating the kids in our congregations—the very children who will inherit the church. Good Christians work all day and then in the evenings volunteer to hold babies in the nursery so young mothers can have a few moments of fellowship. Good Christians show up when it's not convenient. They meet needs too small, too private, or too humiliating to appear on the pastoral staff's radar. As a group, they aren't very loud or showy. They don't have time to storm the castle because they are in the basement holding the castle together. Good Christians, as a tribe, are accurately described as *good* people.

But could we be accurately described as *God* people?

Ouch, I know. But let's take a look at the numbers. If we pause for a moment amid all we're doing and assess the data, we can see our strategy is not working.

According to polls,[1] most people in the United States identify themselves as Christian. Nearly three out of four Americans[2] on the bus consider heaven their ultimate destination, via the work of Jesus. My own church parking lot is packed on any given Sunday, unless the Seahawks are in the playoffs. On Christmas and Easter, it's almost impossible to park anywhere near the building. The bus feels full.

But if roughly 70 percent of Americans claim a faith that promotes unity, selflessness, and all-conquering love, then why is our country such a mess?

---

1 "ABC News Beliefnet Poll, 2001," The Association of Religion Data Archives, https://www.thearda.com.

2 "America's Changing Religious Landscape," Pew Research Center's Religion & Public Life Project, February 12, 2021, https://www.pewforum.org/2015/05/12/americas-changing-religious-landscape/.

Granted, not everyone sporting the jersey plays in the game. For the sake of simplicity, let's eliminate folks with questionable commitment levels. All the seekers and all the sinners dragged to church by someone else—you are dismissed. To make the data more pure, let's vote the C&E crowd—Christmas and Easter—off the island as well. No need to save seats now. And what about church members who only attend occasionally? Well, we can't really build a program on their shoulders, so we won't count them either.

Once the dust clears around the exit doors, what are the numbers? Forty percent of Americans claim regular church attendance, but when measured against actual church attendance data, the number is cut in half. This research sheds light on two interesting facts. First, half of us lie to pollsters. Second, this is how two-thousand-seat auditoriums can hold a congregation of ten thousand.

For a country that identifies itself as Christian, there seems to be considerable vagueness on what behaviors constitute living as a Christian. Ignore the mind-blowing fact that more than half the people who identify themselves as Christian aren't actually populating the Christian church. That might be a book for someone else to write. I'm focused on the roughly 20 percent we would call *doers*. That's the demographic of Good Christians.

At first glance, it seems unfair to say that the 20 percent with their cheeks in the seat are fake. And for years, I was defensive if anyone questioned my authenticity. So let's fly to cruising altitude for a higher vantage point before we get personal.

First things first. We are salt. God calls his followers "the salt of the earth."

Sounds good. But what does that mean? Most Americans use a saltshaker to make things taste better. Is this our job as Christ-followers—to make the world more palatable? Are we here to transform good things into better things? To sprinkle ourselves around and make everyone's day just a little bit tastier?

For those of us not listening in seventh-grade science class, let's review. Salt is a change agent. It has a job—*changing things*.

One time my brother made a favorite family soup recipe, and my dad told him, "You can never add too much salt." Being a literal-minded chef, my brother poured in two cups. The inedible result is a culinary disaster his siblings delight in reminiscing about annually.

If I offered you a dish that was 20 percent salt, would you eat it?

No. Because salt does powerful work. A little bit goes a long, long way. In the presence of salt, bacteria cannot grow. Salt not only evaporates the environment that fosters bacteria, but it also attacks microbes, interrupting their enzymes and altering their DNA. If something is made up of 20 percent salt, no bacteria could survive. When doing its job, salt is an unstoppable force.

Umm.

This begs a question. If the devoted, lifelong followers of Christ—those tasked by God to be like salt—comprise 20 percent of our communities, why are we not the most unstoppable force of goodness in the world today? If the salt was acting as salt should, eliminating decay and altering the cellular makeup of any entity that stood opposed to its properties, wouldn't the Christian church be the most effective source of comfort, love, and hope in a dark and dying world?

Let's circle back to Jesus's words: "You are the salt of the earth. But if the salt loses its saltiness, how can it be made salty again? It is no longer good for anything, except to be thrown out and trampled underfoot" (Matthew 5:13).

Gulp. Don't look now, but I'm pretty sure this verse is saying something to the Good Christian.

Hold on, Harriet. I know what you're thinking. Why am I using feminine pronouns to describe Good Christians? What about the Good Christian Guys? Good question. The sickness is not exclusive to women. It affects us all. There are two main reasons I'm talking to my girls here. First, I'm a woman. I know, very illuminating. But it's true. I've grown up and old in this culture. I've spent the majority of time in church with other women. I am most qualified to speak to my own gender. Men have their own stuff to work on. Maybe more stuff than women—suddenly, a giant *amen* erupts from the crowd—but that's their journey. This is mine.

Second, I'm speaking to the majority of the church. Women *out church* men. A religious landscape study completed by the Pew Research Center indicates that across mainstream denominations, more women attend church than men. And more of us are sure of why we come to church in the first place. Sixty-nine percent of women who attend church state that they are "absolutely certain they believe in God," compared to 57 percent of men.[3] We attend church more regularly because we make it a priority. A whopping 60 percent of women rate church as "very important," compared to 40 percent of men. And the list goes on. We pray more. We read the Bible more. We volunteer more. I wasn't kidding when I said most church programs are built on the backs of the Good Christian woman. We're the worker bees. We are, to a great extent, the faithful.

Why, then, is our world in such a mess? Families are falling apart. Politics are unbearable. War continues to ravage huge portions of the planet. Poverty grows and loneliness consumes. Is it just me, or is the trip to Walmart getting to be a downright meaner experience every week? We've lost our ability to tolerate each other. Just this week there was a video on my Facebook feed of a woman being called horrific names because she was wearing a hijab. She was ordering chicken in a fast-food joint. Really? We can't even order chicken without hating each other?

All this is happening. The world grows darker and colder as many of us collectively slip farther from the God who loves us. And still, I show up for my shift in the church nursery. Every. Blessed. Sunday.

But hang in there with me. I'm simply wondering, not condemning. What are we doing? Why are we doing it? And why are we still doing it if our strategy isn't really working?

---

3 Dalia Fahmy, "Christian Women in the U.S. More Religious than Their Male Counterparts," Pew Research Center, September 10, 2020. https://www.pewresearch.org/fact-tank/2018/04/06/christian-women-in-the-u-s-are-more-religious-than-their-male-counterparts/.

And so I started collecting data on my fellow worker bees and myself. Like a field researcher lying in the mud beneath the ferns so as to not disturb the mountain gorillas, I stood frozen in the ladies' room and absorbed the language of the culture. I volunteered to bring coffee to every event so I could listen to the hum of the hive as they frenetically moved tables and shuffled chairs. My unscientific research yielded a consortium of commonly held beliefs about Good Christians. And here are my notes from the field.

"Good Christians volunteer for everything because it makes them feel good. They get an emotional kickback from it." There is some merit to this argument. It does feel good to serve. It's a bonus of God's design. As we pour into others, we ourselves are filled. However, any good thing can be corrupted. Often we use service as a salve to cover emptiness, loneliness, or other pain too deep to name. Overworking can be a way of underthinking. Service connects us with the God who meets all our needs. When our act of service is twisted—consciously or subconsciously—to meet our own needs, that's when fake happens.

"Good Christians volunteer for everything because they're control freaks." Again, some truth here. I was and still am a control freak. I can't help it; it's a byproduct of my awesome brain. You're welcome, people. God gave me a massive creative streak. The parts of my brain that should be holding on to my PIN numbers and passwords have been commandeered by my need to create. My desire to meet the need is a clear catalyst for overwork. But then my desire to be in charge gets in there as well. If I'm going to help, we might as well do it my way. Just saying.

Thus far, my research indicates that Good Christian motives are complicated. However, it appears the lack of people willing to work in the church is a driving concern for the Good Christian. Simply put, no one else is volunteering. The harvest is plentiful, but the workers are few. This logic appears to hold up. Or does it?

When the same gaggle of Good Christians pops up again and again in the cycle of congregational life, this could be communicating a need for help. However, often the message heard is the exact opposite. Anyone not currently serving might assume his or her gifts aren't needed. If the first-string players keep to their playbook, the new recruits could believe that new plays and players aren't wanted on the team.

"Good Christians are saints. They are at a higher level than most." Clearly, it must be said that some Good Christians are the real deal. I think about all the women I have served alongside, and it's clear some were dialed in on a different wavelength. Their joy was unrelated to the outcome of the potluck. Their peace was relatively consistent. You could sense the roots went deep. I envied them. I wanted to know how they had found this place of peace. What did they know? How did they get there? And they tried to answer my questions, but their words sounded like a list of behaviors all too familiar to me. Yep, already tried that.

Basically, my field research indicated that most of us were poseurs. We knew the right words, and we stood in the right places. But when push came to shove, we were pushing and shoving just like everyone else. We weren't becoming new creations. Mostly, we were becoming tired.

My experience as a Good Christian was primarily thinly veiled exhaustion. Always wondering how I would get it all done. Most of the time, I thought the miracle was that it *did* get done. One more women's breakfast pulled off. Another year of vacation Bible school in the books. Survived Holy Week again. Praise be to God. But every year took more than it gave, and joy was elusive.

As time marched along, the fatigue seeped deep into my soul. Gradually, Bible verses that had always made sense seemed less solid. A classic example is,

> But he said to me, "My grace is sufficient for you, for my power is made perfect in weakness." Therefore I will boast all the more gladly about my weaknesses, so that Christ's power may rest on me. That is why, for Christ's sake, I delight in weaknesses, in insults, in hardships, in persecutions, in difficulties. For when I am weak, then I am strong. (2 Corinthians 12:9–10)

Come on, now. Delighting in weaknesses and insults? Excuse me, but that's just not doable. Of course, I know the church answer. We depend upon God for our strength. God does what we cannot do. The less we can do, the more God will do. Got it. Remember, I've been in church twice a week for forty-odd years. That's roughly 4,160 services. At least some of the time I was listening.

But here's the scoop. I couldn't make myself do it. I couldn't make myself delight in insults. And it wasn't from lack of effort. I would pray and pace and journal. I would turn the other cheek. And when that didn't work, I would gossip in the form of prayer requests across half of the congregation. But no matter what I tried, I couldn't delight when insulted.

The longer I lived, the more I worked. And the greater the mismatch grew between what I read or thought I believed and what I experienced. I am a fairly intelligent person. It bothered me somewhere in the deeper levels of my psyche that my code of conduct didn't yield the promised results. Most often, worry trumped peace. Restlessness trumped joy. And insecurity always trumped confidence. What's a Good Christian to do?

I tried talking to the pastor and his wife. I tried talking to my Bible study teacher and respected sisters in Christ. It was always an incredibly awkward conversation. How should I word it—*I'm not as happy as I think I should be*?

Really? You aren't as happy or peaceful or content as you think you should be?

Alert the prayer chain.

I fumbled around my questions. How? How do you get to the point where you obey without thinking about obeying? When? When does the easy yoke actually start feeling easy? Where? Where in the Bible does it explain how the apostle Paul became able to delight in the face of insults? Because we never do a Bible study on those things. I would definitely sign up. Actually, I always sign up, but I would really *want* to sign up if someone could tell me how to feel the joy of the

Lord that brings strength in the middle of downtown Disneyland as my three-year-old screams curse words at my mother-in-law.

My pastors. My teachers. My friends. Oh, so patient. Oh, so kind. The answer always sounded so simple. It was some version of getting *right with God*. The getting-right process usually involved devotional reading, prayer, and a somber meditation on Proverbs 31.

And so I would try. I doubled down on the devotional, stuck Bible verses to the bathroom mirror, and practiced saying nice things to my husband when he came into the room. I wanted to narrow the gap between what I believed to be true about God and what I experienced of God in my daily life. But eventually, I'd get busy or distracted or lazy—or some great combination of the three—and fall off the getting *right with God* wagon.

I didn't blame God for my lack of connection. I was sure the problem was over here on my side of the line. But no matter what I tried, I couldn't get that internal change the Bible talked about. Highly discouraged, I'd fizzle and poop out. Give up again. I was a Good Christian who couldn't actually *do* the Good Christian things consistently. Not when my own agenda was so appealing. Given the poor yield on the promises of God, there was little logical incentive to keep up with Good Christian behaviors in the privacy of my own home.

However, I didn't want to throw in the towel. So much of my identity was made up of church life. Instead, I used external supports to promote internal habits. I used the structure of attending Bible study to make myself read the Bible. I used the routine of church meetings, meals, and ever-present moments of crisis to make myself pray. I used the volunteering efforts involved in furthering the kingdom to distract myself from my lack of actual *progress* in the kingdom.

The problem with this strategy is that it comes to a dead end. When we aren't growing internally with Christ, the gap between what we profess to believe and what we experience will ever widen until we just sort of shrivel up. And then we either drop out of the whole church thing or—more dangerously—join the hordes of walking dead that clog our churches every Sunday.

So in reviewing our discussion so far, let's acknowledge that Good Christians do lots of good things for the church and the world at large. Many programs are run by overworked and under acknowledged women who had full plates before even driving into the church parking lot. Let's also agree that not all women in the church are Good Christians. Some women are seeking, some are checked out, and others have legitimately found the key to unlock the resources of heaven in real time.

Within the category of Good Christian, there is a diverse group of women who actively participate in church life with a wide-ranging level of uncertainty or disappointment as to why they don't feel more of God's strength in the daily machinations of life. They typically blame themselves for a lack of connection or inner transformation. Frequently, they use external programs to propel inner habits—Bible study, prayer groups, Sunday school—and have difficulty sustaining habits that promote inner transformation without external support. And finally, Good Christians frequently overwork as a means of coping or distracting themselves from the pain of the gap—the gap between what they profess to believe and what they actually experience on a daily basis.

Sounds like the salt has got some issues.

And the problem with salt is that if it's not doing what it's designed to do, it's not good for much else.

> To the angel of the church in Laodicea write: These are the words of the Amen, the faithful and true witness, the ruler of God's creation. I know your deeds, that you are neither cold nor hot. I wish you were either one or the other! So, because you are lukewarm—neither hot nor cold—I am about to spit you out of my mouth. (Revelation 3:14–16)

Hmm. It appears working furiously to further the kingdom, without allowing God to transform us into the likeness of Jesus, isn't an option in God's playbook. These verses are aimed right at salt that has lost its saltiness. You heard me, Good Christians. It's aimed at us.

But wait. Didn't we agree that Good Christians do lots of good stuff? Yes. The verse didn't say, "I see your bad deeds." It says *deeds*. It means *stuff*. Doesn't matter what stuff we do when our hearts are lukewarm. It's not enough to do good stuff. We must be fully committed to God, seeking out the life that brings life, and becoming a new creation. Otherwise, we are lukewarm and—in the words of Holy Scripture—vomit-worthy.

Sounds harsh, right? But God isn't vague about this. Lukewarm is unacceptable. There's no room on the team for those simply wearing the jersey. We must be all in. And the only measure that I can find in Scripture of *all in* is inner transformation.

It's not what we do. It's who we are becoming.

Our behavior is simply behavior. God only ever seems concerned with the motivation of the heart. After healing a blind man, Jesus calls out the Pharisees for knowing and doing the right thing without transforming internally:

> Jesus said, "For judgment I have come into this world, so that the blind will see and those who see will become blind." Some Pharisees who were with him heard him say this and asked, "What? Are we blind too?" Jesus said, "If you were blind, you would not be guilty of sin; but now that you claim you can see, your guilt remains." (John 9:39–41)

Nope. Not vague.

Because lukewarm is dangerous. It dumbs down the difference between Christ-followers and everyone else. It breeds confusion. Lukewarm fosters wolves in sheep's clothing. It makes church no different from junior high or the workplace or Club Med. Depending on the church.

Turns out that science agrees with Jesus. Lukewarm is dangerous in fighting disease. When bacteria are in a lukewarm environment, the conditions outside the cells are equal to the conditions inside the cells. So the disease can multiply at a rapid rate. Lukewarm food becomes poisonous quickly. And lukewarm coffee? Enough said.

The problem with lukewarm is that it allows us to profess a certain belief while functionally acting on another belief. We can profess God as sovereign and in charge of all things yet rarely consult him on where we spend our money or where we work or even whom we keep as friends. When we're lukewarm, God can busy himself with the universe while we busy ourselves on Instagram. Lukewarm followers can say—usually to our children—that it's who we are on the inside that counts, while themselves ruthlessly conforming to insane societal norms of youthful appearance and physical attraction.

Naegleria fowleri is a fancy science name for "brain-eating amoeba." True story. These suckers live in fresh water that is—wait for it—lukewarm. When my family went to Yellowstone National Park, there were posted signs near the hot springs warning tourists to Swim at Your Own Risk. These brain-eating amoebas can invade a body through the nose, eyes, ears, or even a tiny cut on the foot. And then—death.

Care to guess the natural enemy of *Naegleria fowleri*? Yep. Salt.

Brain-eating amoebas have invaded the church. And unsalted salt does nothing to save it from the menace of lukewarm faith. The invisible amoebas subtly mix legalistic rule following and lazy grace grubbing. We reduce our faith to a to-do list and justify berating our fellow life travelers when they fail to check a box. We use our zombie-like understanding of grace to excuse sick and perverse behaviors with the statement "God will forgive me." We stand in church every Sunday, practically bathing in the life-giving words of Scripture, and then cut each other off in the parking lot.

Jesus was describing this when he spoke of the house built on sand. Lukewarm seems to work until it doesn't. Here comes the storm—cancer, car accident, unemployment, divorce—and then what? We can't find the power source. Because we spent so much time living in our own strength, while simultaneously consenting that God alone is powerful.

Jesus would spit us out of his mouth. Lukewarm is killing us. When we accept a form of Christianity that doesn't make internal transformation an absolute requirement, we strip ourselves of the power of God. We severely dim—if not extinguish—our light. And we settle for sitting in darkness while also believing that light exists somewhere.

Salt changes things. In the presence of salt, no zombie-producing amoeba could survive. Salt attacks bacteria at the DNA level. Want to know how much salt is needed to utterly defeat amoebic invaders?

Twenty percent.

The irony. That's the exact percentage of Good Christian attendance.

We can't keep doing what we're doing. It's not okay to do the good stuff without knowing our own motivation. Whom are we serving? If the Bible verses don't make sense—if they are not demonstrated practically by the actual life we're living—we must stop. If God's promises are not flowing in and out of our day like oxygen, how can we trust him? We must fight our internal zombie and reattach grace to thought. We have to go back. We can't let the pressures of life—and the complications of being human—prevent us from transformation.

Transformation—and transformation alone—is evidence of *right with God.*

Good Christians everywhere, listen up. It's time to fish or cut bait. Choose a side and get in the game. We can't continue to do good things for wrong or unclear reasons. Allowing God to access our inner self and transform it bit by bit into the image of Christ must be our primary goal. We can't simply *do* what Jesus would do. We must think like Jesus, breathe like Jesus, and feel like Jesus.

Our current modus operandi isn't working. If 20 percent of America believes we're salt, then we've clearly lost our saltiness. We must do church, do life, and do the thing—whatever the thing is—with Jesus as our all-consuming guide.

The day I demolished my coffee mug, I didn't really know what I was doing. I've always had a flair for the dramatic. But the chasm between what I professed to believe and what I actually experienced felt so wide I nearly fell in.

I didn't understand I was lukewarm. I didn't consider myself a Good Christian. All I knew was that I was a tired, disillusioned, and somewhat bitter girl. The train had jumped the track, and I was overwhelmingly aware that forward movement was impossible with the current trajectory. So I headed back. Turns out I had missed something.

Something huge. Enormous.

Smashing my sweet little mug was an epic moment—a death knell of sorts. I didn't know it then, but it was the beginning of killing off my Good Christian self in pursuit of something better and bigger. Fabulously free yet slavishly devoted. God doesn't want Good Christians. He's got another word for what he wants.

Ezer.

CHAPTER 3

Learning to Unsee

Jesus and the early Apostles preached a salvation radically different from the kind of salvation being preached today. They spoke of a life in the kingdom of God encompassing all of human existence, both here and hereafter. The circumference of their message embraces 360 degrees.

—Richard Foster, "Salvation Is for Life," *Theology Today*

THERE IS AN INFAMOUS FAMILY PORTRAIT TAKEN WHEN I WAS about four. Everyone is smiling at the camera in their gloriously loud seventies attire. But I'm rotated ninety degrees from the camera and staring at the wall. It's rather prophetic. I have a gift for sort of missing the main event.

Case in point. In 1986, the United States sent a teacher, Christa McAuliffe, into space. It was a huge deal. It was also a huge deal to skip language arts class in favor of watching the broadcasted launching. Mrs. Barry slowly wheeled a large box-shaped television, strapped atop a tall cart that swayed precariously with every bump or jostle, into our room. We were fascinated, not so much by what we'd see on the screen but by Mrs. Barry struggling with the uncooperative cart.

Unfortunately, when I get really excited, I often need to visit the restroom. I blame my mother's side of the family for my microscopic bladder. Grabbing the hall pass, I ran to and from the bathroom as fast as the school rules would allow. When I returned to the classroom, my friends were pale and many were weeping. Even venerable old Mrs. Barry had tears on her cheeks. I glanced at what appeared to be benign, puffy clouds on the screen and attempted to comprehend the colossal shift. It felt like the world had changed and I missed it. Because my eyes had always seen clouds, I couldn't see an exploded space shuttle.

When the World Trade Center fell many years later, I was watching *Clifford the Big Red Dog* with my babies. I had no idea the entire world had collectively gasped in horror. My morning on September 11, 2001, was filled with the perpetually positive Emily Elizabeth.

It's a pattern. So when I examine my path to becoming a Good Christian, it shouldn't be surprising that I somehow missed the main thing. The big picture.

I misunderstood the *gospel.*

Can we pause for a moment and just let that sink in? I missed the main point of the entire Bible. I misunderstood it. I lived in a state of confusion while attending church over four thousand times. Astounding.

As a little peep sitting in the pew, here's what I heard. Adam and Eve were created by God. God loved them, and they loved him. But they were fooled into disobedience, and everything was wrecked by sin. Now Adam would have to sweat, and childbirth would involve stirrups. And humankind can't go to heaven because of this sin. Instead, we will go to hell, which is horrible torture. But the good news is that God loved us very much, and he sent his son Jesus to receive our punishment. And because we are Christians, we live differently. We love the unlovable. We live unselfishly. We do this because we love God, and when we die, we go to heaven to live forever in paradise. The end.

Salvation—what an amazing gift. What a good, good God. That he would love me so much, even in my sinful state, to send Jesus to take my place—to pay for my sin and the sins of the world.

But therein lies the crucial disconnect—loving Jesus *because he took my place.* Wait, Marion, don't drop the book just yet. The problem with focusing solely on the forgiveness of sins is that we learn to love God because he gives us something. Jesus becomes our ticket. Our love for him is dependent on his act of dying for us. Everything is reduced to a transaction. I want him because he saved me.

We need to understand the roles a little better. Jesus loved *us* enough to die in our place, even though we didn't deserve that kindness. And we love *God* because we believe he *is* God. He's our only hope, and we put all of our trust in him. We have nothing else to live for.

But if salvation is simply an agreement in which I believe Jesus made it possible for me to go to heaven, then there's really nothing else for me to do.

And that is why the green page is so blessedly impossible.

You know the green page. The one in the *Wordless Book*. No? Okay, a short review. The *Wordless Book* is a highly effective evangelism tool with no words—hence the clever name—to explain the steps of salvation to children. Different colors represent different steps of understanding our need for a Savior. The black page represents sin. Red is Jesus's blood. Yellow, heaven. And then, growth.

Growth is the green page. After the yellow page, where we are assured of salvation and our entrance into heaven, is the green page of growth. Before we go to heaven, God wants us to grow in our knowledge and understanding of him. The more we know God, the easier it is to trust him, and the easier it is to do the impossibly hard things we are tasked with doing. Like not smacking my brother back when he smacks me.

To my adolescent brain, the green page appeared optional. If I had the ticket, I was in, right? I could do a great job—or a terrible job—at the green page. Obviously, I should *desire* to grow because growth is good. But really, if I had the ticket, I was through the gate.

Man. What an awesome gift.

The green page felt like a teacher assigning optional homework. Umm, no thanks. Because it's *optional*.

As I matured, my understanding changed. I loved God and wanted to give the green page a go, but our relationship was still based on a transaction. I loved him because of what he'd done for me. So my behavior was always based on quid pro quo. He saved me from my sin, therefore I will organize the church potluck. Or volunteer in the nursery. Or fulfill any number of Good Christian commitments. But when my relationship with God was based on this premise, the outcome felt unsure. I had to hold up my end of the bargain—and if I didn't, it was impossible not to imagine that God's love might waver.

When we focus on Jesus forgiving our sins, salvation becomes a transaction that is completed rather than a process that is initiated.

I'm a total fan of Dallas Willard. And John Ortberg, Tim Keller, and Carolyn Custis James. They write about these things too. Many Christian leaders are puzzled by the general ineptness of the massive Western church.

And Dallas Willard was instrumental in helping me find the origin of the Good Christian. In his book, *The Spirit of the Disciplines,* he has a chapter entitled, "Salvation Is a Life" in which he wondered, "Why is it that we look upon our salvation as a moment that began our religious life instead of the daily life we receive from God?"[4]

Yeah. Good question. My fundamental understanding was once saved, Christians should live a godly life.

But hold the phone. That's not what Dallas said. Salvation is a *life*. A new life. A life that Jesus brings.

The first step of salvation is to unequivocally surrender to God. To put myself—all of me, all my resources, even the breath in my lungs—on God's team and allow him to be the Coach. I bet my entire life on the belief that God is *the One*. The answer to every question. The amazing, astounding, loving source of all power. When I ask God for salvation, I understand that everything I am and all I ever hope to be now belongs to him.

And I dedicate myself to a life in his shadow. A life of following, a life of fellowship, a life of never being alone with my own thoughts. Salvation, rightly translated, is a life.

---

4 Dallas Willard, "Salvation Is a Life," in *The Spirit of the Disciplines: Understanding How God Changes Lives*, (Grand Rapids, MI: Family Christian Press, 2001), 28.

The entirety of my life's ambition is to be with Jesus and to grow more and more like him. I become increasingly aware of the magnitude of what Jesus has done for me—his sacrifice that enables me to receive new life—and this growing knowledge of his character increases my love for him. I love him because he is my God. My Sun. My Universe.

C. S. Lewis put it plainly: "I believe in Christianity as I believe that the Sun has risen, not only because I see it but because by it, I see everything else."[5]

So Jesus places his team jersey on me so I can play. This is salvation.

But often we teach and believe the opposite. When we focus solely on the forgiveness of sins, we say Jesus allowed you on the team. Done. Nothing more is required. And this creates an environment where lukewarm is possible. We can profess one thing while functionally believing another.

This may sound confusing and borderline heretical. But here's the deal. We've got to read the Bible for what it says. The gospel—the good news that Jesus preached—is about entering the kingdom. Entering a new life. His work on the cross is the *entrance,* not the destination. That is what Paul talks about when he says run the race. Fight the good fight. Grab the part of life that is really life. Why is Paul straining? I mean, if he has the ticket. He's either overworking or we've missed something. The purpose of Jesus's death on the cross was not to establish a minimal entrance requirement for the pearly gates.

But that's what many believe. Pray the prayer, and you're in. That's what I heard, and that's why the green page was the bane of my existence.

Because while I had fully accepted Jesus's offer as my ticket to escape sin and enter heaven, I hadn't accepted the notion that God wanted all of me—every single cell, every thought, every wish. I didn't know who God truly was. I didn't relate to him as a dearly adored child approaching a father. I didn't love him because of his holiness. I loved him because I didn't want to go to hell.

---

5 C. S. Lewis, *They Asked for a Paper,* (Geoffrey Bles Ltd., 1962), 164–65.

And when we believe that way—when we allow that to be the foundation of our faith—we remain sovereign unto ourselves. We remain in a relationship that looks more like a business deal. We disconnect our daily behavior from our religious beliefs, or we participate in activities to serve God as a form of earning grace. Many, many people view Christianity as a safety net. Fire insurance. Irrelevant to everyday life. I don't need to drive my car with Jesus. Or browse on my phone with Jesus. I only truly need Jesus to open the escape hatch.

And now we see how salt can lack saltiness. There's no supernatural element to our lives—only assurance of the final destination. We continue vying for control of our lives. And then transformation—the evidence that proves *right with God*—is elusive, if not downright impossible.

Sigh. This may sound like semantics mumbo jumbo, but it's so foundational. Until we know who God is, we can't identify ourselves in him. Until we identify ourselves in him, we can't have confidence. And without confidence, we have no consistent access to all the resources of heaven.

There are a million and one ways to misunderstand what I've just said. It takes time to learn to see a new thing. The first two times I read Dallas Willard's *The Spirit of the Disciplines*, I chucked the book at the wall every couple of pages. My frustration was so regular that my husband began to expect flying literature right before bed. As the book sailed over his head and smacked the wall, he'd turn out the light and sleepily mutter, "Good night, Dallas."

What drove me crazy was that I could see something I didn't have. It was like looking across a ravine at a parallel trail. I was headed in the right direction but on the wrong path. And I wanted to be on the right path, but sweet baby Moses, I didn't have a map.

It felt like walking into Mrs. Barry's classroom and realizing I'd missed something big. But none of the data seemed to compute. I just saw fluffy clouds. I didn't have a mental or visual category for a space shuttle explosion.

And similarly, reading Willard's words presented so much confusion to my current state of Christian life that it became clear I needed a paradigm shift.

The voice of my former professor, Dr. Mayhee, echoed in my head. "Until you unsee what you were taught, you can't see what no one else sees." Dr. Mayhee always said stuff like that. He was exceptionally tall and the very definition of *slow talker.* I was bored in graduate school because it was graduate school and nothing was allowed to be remotely fun. Scholars pay for knowledge, not fun. But Dr. Mayhee, with his slow-talking ways, appeared to enjoy the moment of teaching.

He leaned against the whiteboard and paused before speaking. Then he said, "The future belongs to the one who can unsee what is seen, so they can see what no one else sees." He sounded like Dr. Seuss. A very relaxed Dr. Seuss. Did I mention the slow talking?

But then he told the story of Chester Carlson. Chester was a classic underdog who developed the process to create a rough image using electrostatic energy. A very crude form of photography. Who would want such a thing? It was a far cry from the industry's standard of replicating images. But Chester was able to unsee the ugly image and instead see an amazingly simple way to reproduce written documents. Twenty companies turned him down before one finally took a chance on Chester. And on the basis of his innovation, Xerox was born.

The world shifted in response to Chester's vision. Why would we use carbon paper to duplicate documents? Why would we do this the old way? The new way is the only way. Paradigm shifted.

Jesus himself brought a paradigm shift of cataclysmic proportions. He came as a fulfillment of the law. He didn't simply find a loophole for us to slip through. By meeting the standard established by the law, Jesus fulfilled the obligation of the law while simultaneously raising the standard. Moving forward, it wouldn't be enough to do the right thing with impure or confused motives. Now—and forever—it would be the motivation of the heart that qualifies behavior. The state of the heart is the new measurement of success. Not the behavior. Not even what the behavior accomplishes.

Jesus explains this, saying, "Small is the gate and narrow the road that leads to life, and only a few find it" (Matthew 7:14). Why would the gate be narrow if what he offered was a freely given ticket for entrance into heaven? The gate is small. The road is narrow. We aren't going to effortlessly stumble into glory.

But often, we preach the entirety of Christian faith as a free transaction that requires nothing from the sinner. We equate putting our trust in Jesus with the effort needed to fall out of bed. The fact that more sinners don't gobble up the gospel we offer appears to reinforce the human race's status as stupid sheep.

But wait, there's more.

Jesus goes on to speak against false prophets, warning that they come in sheep's clothing but are actually ferocious wolves. As a child, I imagined these false prophets as sort of reverse missionaries. People hired by the devil to go wreck things inside the church. They would be easy to spot because their wolfishness would stick out under the sheep's clothing. Like, we could tell they weren't real Christians because their behavior would tip us off. Maybe they would smoke a cig in the sanctuary.

Part of my thinking was right. The wolf parts do stick out. Remember, transformation is the only indicator of *right with God*. If we are not slavishly devoted to having Jesus influence everything we do—all day, every day—then it's time to look under our wool. My journey indicates that Good Christian is synonymous with wolf more times than not.

Take a breath, Marge. Good Christians are rarely purposefully killing the church. A wolf doesn't know it's ferocious. It doesn't feel evil or mean. It's just a wolf. The problem with being a Good Christian, rather than a surrendered child, is that we're ignorant of our true heart condition. We don't desire to be *with* and *like* God. Our relationship with God doesn't inform all of our deeds, all of our advice, and all of our love. With the very best intentions, we inform ourselves. When we come inside the church and stay there without *transforming*, we continue to play by all the rules of the world. We hurt more than we help. When salt loses its saltiness, it doesn't offer the world anything different from their current daily experiences. People inside the church are just as anxious, tired, selfish, fearful, prideful, and lonely as the world outside the church. So if the reason for coming to church is a ticket to heaven, what is the reason for staying?

Jesus goes on to speak some of the saddest words in the entirety of Holy Scripture:

> Not everyone who says to me, "Lord, Lord," will enter the kingdom of heaven, but only the one who does the will of my Father who is in heaven. Many will say to me on that day, "Lord, Lord, did we not prophesy in your name and in your name drive out demons and in your name perform many miracles?" Then I will tell them plainly, "I never knew you. Away from me, you evildoers!" (Matthew 7:21–23)

Devastating.

Clearly, the people standing in front of Jesus believed they were in. If our good works aren't indicators of being *right with God*, then loads of us are on sinking ships.

Jesus was saying that the inside life must match the outside life for the outside life to count at all.

Here's the kicker. I used my behavior to attempt to rule my heart. Scripture clearly teaches the reverse—the heart will always rule behavior—so my math was obviously wrong. When I examined my faith, I could see a God who loved me. And I loved him. But there were all these verses that didn't make sense. One of my biggest sticklers was joy. The Bible talks about joy as if it's a real thing to experience in real life. Joy described in Scripture isn't dependent upon circumstances. This joy doesn't come and go according to the whims of neurochemistry or the amount of caffeine in one's system.

And I wanted this joy. Badly.

So I would set out after it. Study, read, memorize, pray. And I felt better doing all these things. But I'm lazy and inconsistent, and try as I might, I didn't experience this joy. So then I felt guilty and slid further into my Good Christian ways. It was just mentally easier to do things without the conviction of experience than to constantly question why my experience didn't live up to what God offered.

Need examples? What about those crazy verses that ask us to turn the other cheek so that we have the blessing of being punched again? Or those passages about loving our enemies? I absolutely couldn't get my innards to behave. I might do or even say the right thing, but believe me, a different script was playing inside my head. Usually involving colorful language.

So there I was. Pretty sure I was one of those trees in Scripture that thought she was in the cherry orchard but kept churning out crab apples. I looked under my wool and saw a wolf. A person who embraced God's love yet rejected his Lordship in daily life.

Paul warns Timothy about people like me. People who have a form of godliness without life-changing power. I imagine the conversation between the mentor and his mentee: "Tim, listen to me. I don't care how understaffed the nursery is. When you work with wolves, someone's gonna get hurt. Our job is to protect the flock. Don't have anything to do with that Good Christian."

Paul's direct order was to not associate with me.

I felt miserable. And finally came to the point where I was willing to walk away from the church rather than remain fake inside it.

God loved me. I was overwhelmed with a sense that he still wanted me. But I was no longer willing to claim a faith that promised supernatural, transformational power while my life was filled with so much fear, anxiety, and doubt. Surely, I'd missed something. I had to unsee what I'd always seen so that I could see what I'd never seen. And I begged God for help.

I went through the Bible and underlined every single time the word *power* was used. I read a lot of books written by smart people and then talked with others who could help me understand what the smart people were saying. And it all sort of lumped into one idea. It wasn't about working harder; it was about surrendering more.

What does that mean? Well, if we go all the way back to little Hollylu sitting in the pew, looking at the *Wordless Book*, it means this: *autonomy is not on the table.*

Little Hollylu blinks.

Yes, you understand your need for saving. You understand the sin problem. And you see there's a God who loves you so much, and he wants you choose him. But here's what you also need to know. You aren't choosing whether you want God to be the boss or you want to stay in charge of your life yourself. You can never be the boss of your life. Rather, you have two masters to choose between. Your first option is to serve the world. This can look very appealing. It has glitz, glamour, and Mountain Dew. But it's a cruel master. You will always try to measure up, but you never will. The world will take you and love you only for what you have to offer. And eventually, it will leave you empty and alone.

Your other option is to ask God to rescue you out of this pit of hopelessness, and he will adopt you into his family. But that means God is the boss. You must enslave yourself to following him and becoming like him. You are not your own, and you never will be. But he is so incredible that the more you slave away for him, the freer you will become. He will overwhelm you with his joy and delight you with the tenderness of his care. He will never leave you. He will always love you. He could never love you more or less than he already does. And you will come *alive.*

So what's your choice? A slave to the enticement of sin—with its illusion of control—in a crumbling and fake world?

Or a slave to God? A kind and loving Master who offers life that is full of joy and strength and community.

Remember, being your own boss is *not* an option.

This is what I want little Hollylu—and everyone—to know. Self-governance isn't a choice. Living life your way, calling your own shots, or being the captain of your fate. Sorry, peeps, it doesn't work that way. We're either slaves to our culture or slaves to righteousness. Slavery is a given. Our only choice is the master we serve.

And now we read Jesus's words with better understanding.

> Large crowds were traveling with Jesus, and turning to them he said: "If anyone comes to me and does not hate father and mother, wife and children, brothers and sisters—yes, even their own life—such a person cannot be my disciple. And whoever does not carry their cross and follow me cannot be my disciple.
>
> "Suppose one of you wants to build a tower. Won't you first sit down and estimate the cost to see if you have enough money to complete it? For if you lay the foundation and are not able to finish it, everyone who sees it will ridicule you, saying, 'This person began to build and wasn't able to finish.'
>
> "Or suppose a king is about to go to war against another king. Won't he first sit down and consider whether he is able with ten thousand men to oppose the one coming against him with twenty thousand? If he is not able, he will send a delegation while the other is still a long way off and will ask for terms of peace. In the same way, those of you who do not give up everything you have cannot be my disciples.
>
> "Salt is good, but if it loses its saltiness, how can it be made salty again?" (Luke 14:25–34)

Exactly so.

Suddenly, the large crowds were like, "Hey, what's this strange rabbi talking about? I'm here for the free bread and fish."

Jesus was talking about slavery—slavery to righteousness.

If we bring the idea of total enslavement back to church, we get lots of weird looks. I mean, really. Let's not get carried away. Before we know it, we'll be boycotting cable networks and limiting our caffeine intake.

No thanks.

Americans are wary of anything that restricts our freedom. But that's the illusion—the part we have to unsee. We were never free in that sense. We are created beings rightly compared to sheep. We simply go with the flow of paradigms, gestalts, and worldviews instilled by our culture. We aren't really that evolved beyond junior high. We're just more sophisticatedly blind. We want to fit in, and we will get our identity somewhere, either from God or from the world. And then we'll serve the source of our identity with complete devotion, even if we're ignorant of the process.

So now let's circle the coffee cart back to the understanding of salvation. Jesus came so that we might have life and have it to the full. He is the entrance into the kingdom. And if we reach for it—if we decide God is *the One* and offer our life for him to take—he welcomes us with outrageous joy. He adopts us into his family and calls us his children. We pursue—and fall deeper in love with—a real Person. Our goal is to be completely consumed by him. His thoughts. His feelings. And then we change, or more accurately, he changes us. More and more of the new creation is brought forward.

We must embrace an understanding of the gospel that places emphasis not only on the amazing forgiveness of sins but also on our commitment to enslave ourselves to Christ. And then a life of discipleship is the logical outcome of conversion.

Gulp. I just saw two-thirds of my childhood congregation stand up and walk out of this book because it sounds like *works*. It sounds like grace isn't free. It sounds like we do something to earn our salvation.

That's absolutely not what I mean. We can't and don't save ourselves. But we do say *yes* to the saving. We commit, go all in, and give our life to God. Thus begins an all-consuming apprenticeship to him.

I know what you're thinking: "Good night, Dallas."

But here's the deal. Until I shifted my thinking—until I learned to unsee passive grace—I wasn't able to see active grace. Now, with this understanding of salvation, I became better informed. Righteousness isn't confused with legalism. I understand why buying spiritual fire insurance never seemed to work.

It was never offered.

Inner transformation is the only proof of *right with God*. The reason I kept sliding into Good Christian ways was that my transactional faith was primarily focused on behavior modification. After accepting Christ as my Savior, I continued to serve my desires. My ideas. I continued to be my own ruler. This is how it was possible for me to sing and praise God's name on Sunday morning but then feel abandoned and disillusioned and bail out on the God thing when life got hard. Because all along, I was trusting in myself. My plan. And God was supposed to bless my plan.

The storm came. And it turns out my house was built on sand.

And so my next challenge emerged. Was I willing to live as a slave to Christ? And what did that mean anyway? Did I have to become a monk? Give away my possessions? Stop wearing earrings?

I wasn't interested in behavior modification anymore. I was interested in knowing Jesus so well that I no longer had to *think* about doing the right thing. I wanted the right thing to be my first response. I wanted to live in his shadow. Breathe in his air. And I wanted that *joy*.

Hmm.

I had to rethink discipleship. Discipleship is a tough notion to handle, what with discipline being at the root. But I was done being a wolf.

Shortly after the mug-smashing episode, I came to my ultimate fork in the road. One direction was unbelief. Throw in the towel. Totally cast off religion. The other direction was to abandon my way of thinking about Christianity. Because clearly, the foundation I had was flawed.

Curled up in bed in the middle of the night, I considered all these things. I thought of little Hollylu. I felt the weight of truth. God loved me unconditionally. And a question emerged: Was I willing to love him unconditionally? Standing on the edge of my existential cliff, I prayed.

All right, God. I want to be all in. Teach me to be all in.

I felt like little Samuel standing in the dark.

Deep in my soul, the pearls loosened. My proper beige Good Christian dress disappeared. Now I had new clothes. Not angelic choir robes or a prom dress or even a team jersey.

Jesus held out the clothes of a warrior.

Paradigm shifted.

CHAPTER 4

Helen, Highlighters, and Unsightly Gaps

Never try to teach a pig to sing. It wastes your time, and it annoys the pig.

—Robert Heinlein, *Time Enough for Love: The Lives of Lazarus Long*

THE WORD *DISCIPLESHIP* MAKES ME ANXIOUS.

For some of us who grew up in the church, we've sort of had it with that word. The word, I mean. In fact, the first step in learning to unsee was to make a list of words I vowed never to use again. It was a long list.

Part of building a new paradigm included relabeling everything because some words just represented a whole lot of failure. A classic example is Quiet Time. I will never, ever use that term again. Because reasons.

Surely, I'm not the only one who has colossally failed at having a daily—or any kind of regular—Quiet Time. At age fourteen, I felt responsible for my high school football team losing the state playoffs. Because. Everyone knows if you want heaven to hear your prayers, you'd better be paying the Quiet Time Bill.

The Quiet Time Bill? Yes. The QTB.

Let's go back to Sunday school, shall we? At least, *my* Sunday school, which was amazing. In my church, we didn't skip over parts of the Bible. This was before fancy curricula were invented. There were very few visual aids, and YouTube wasn't even a figment of the imagination. What we had was the Bible, and it was completely groovy. Whatever they were learning upstairs, we learned downstairs. It was so simple compared to what we do today, but wow, talk about knowing the Bible. Before I went off to college and before I started writing Bible studies, I had a scriptural foundation delivered one Sunday at a time until my understanding of the Bible—its flow and beauty—stood beneath me like a fortress.

Thank you, Mrs. Leaders, Mrs. Gowan, and Mrs. Dicks.

Here's the deal. People who accept Christ without fully surrendering their heart—people like me—are the ones weighing down the church. Our filter is imperceptibly yet fundamentally off. We can say and do all the right things without connecting to the right One. Thus, the church—and the relationships within it—can lack salt. Every Christ-follower is on a journey of surrendering the self. The concept of taking up one's cross daily and losing your life so you might gain it looks like a spectrum. Thankfully, I grew up surrounded by genuine saints.

The women who taught my Sunday school lessons were mostly housewives living and dying under the Midwest sun. But they were connected to something eternal. I could hear it when they spoke. Mrs. Gowan was passionately in love with Jesus and particularly good at communicating that love to a group of sticky children who sat captivated at her feet.

Every week she rested the open Bible on her lap. She leaned back, closed her eyes, and told us the story. We were sucked right off the shag carpet and into ancient Palestine. Sunday by Sunday, we marched through the Pentateuch. Invaded Canaan. Watched with frustration as the prophets were ignored again and again. Rejoiced with the coming of our Savior, recoiled at his death, and danced at his resurrection. We spread out the maps with Paul and watched the Word move out of Israel and into the world. We delivered the letters to the churches. And then, with great anticipation, we yearned for the City of Gold.

The stories weren't truncated or dumbed down. We didn't have hand motions or crafts made of neon foam. It was just the Bible. From my very beginning, I found God's story fascinating, beautiful, and complete. And I still do.

I remember sitting on the rug with my brother and friends, digging my fingers into the loops of the shag carpet as Elijah sat on top of his mountain. The pathetically awful King Ahaziah sent a captain, with his regiment of fifty fighting men, up the mountain to make the prophet of God come down.

"Man of God," the captain said to Elijah, "King Ahaziah says, 'You must come down at once.'"

And Elijah, who was an incredibly cool cucumber, basically responded that if he were indeed a man of God, then they were all toast.

Ka-pow! The captain and his fifty men were consumed by fire. We collectively gasped. And eyed each other nervously.

Then the king sent another captain with another regiment of fifty soldiers up the mountain to confront Elijah with the exact same strategy. We cringed. We knew what was likely to happen. Ahaziah was awfully cavalier with the lives of these soldiers.

Zap!

At this point, Mrs. Gowan opened one eye and stared at us children—as we sat there with open mouths—and asked, "What would you do if you were captain number three?"

And my brother responded with profound simplicity, "Switch teams."

This God that we learned about in church was absolutely compelling. Truly astounding. But then I'd leave Sunday school, and the world would do its thing. I wanted to know God like Elijah knew God. But there were a lot of distractions—clothes, boys, books, moon pies. God was like drinking water. It was good for me. But the world had soda pop in a can. It was glow-in-the-dark green and tasted like liquid sugar. Water just couldn't compete.

As I neared junior high, I could feel a widening gap between the truth I'd learned about God and what I experienced in my actual life.

And the gap bothered me. Because I loved God.

Since the day I put my trust in Christ, I felt his unwavering love. And I loved him back. But power? I didn't experience much of God's supernatural strength in the everyday. And I assumed this must be due to my life strategy of not really following. If I'd been able to articulate it, my goal was to remain in the driver's seat. I wanted to seek pleasure and avoid discomfort. If God didn't spare his own followers pain or discomfort—including his only Son—then following God was risky.

In short, my goal was to *not* be Hudson Taylor. Because pain is painful. And all I could see when I looked at the venerable old man, with his long white braid, was suffering.

I wanted to wear God's jersey with no persisting allegiance to the Coach who might make me do hard things. Yep. That would be the gap.

And then I found this gap in my Bible. I actually found it. It's in your Bible too. For those of us who missed the good news in its entirety, there is a cavernous, gaping crevasse between Romans 7 and Romans 8. If you want, you can look now. I'll wait.

Ha! I wouldn't have looked either. I'd wait to see if the author was just going to tell me, because overworking is not my thing. Some call it laziness; others call it efficiency. I've heard it both ways.

Here's the deal. Romans 7 is written by the apostle Paul. He's talking about a regeneration thing—a metamorphosis. Changing from old creature into new creature. It's a process, and it's fraught with setbacks. Why? Because of sin.

Here's what Paul says:

> We know that the law is spiritual; but I am unspiritual, sold as a slave to sin. I do not understand what I do. For what I want to do I do not do, but what I hate I do. And if I do what I do not want to do, I agree that the law is good. As it is, it is no longer I myself who do it, but it is sin living in me. For I know that good itself does not dwell in me, that is, in my sinful nature. For I have the desire to do what is good, but I cannot carry it out. For I do not do the good I want to do, but the evil I do not want to do—this I keep on doing.

> Now if I do what I do not want to do, it is no longer I who do it, but it is sin living in me that does it.
>
> So I find this law at work: Although I want to do good, evil is right there with me. For in my inner being I delight in God's law; but I see another law at work in me, waging war against the law of my mind and making me a prisoner of the law of sin at work within me. What a wretched man I am! Who will rescue me from this body that is subject to death? (Romans 7:14–24)

True confession. I read Romans 7 approximately 743 times before it started making any sense. It's a doozy. Paul's got his own Dr. Seuss rhythm going on here. But what is immediately understandable is that Paul spoke in the *present tense*. And he isn't some bum lying in an alley somewhere. This is the apostle Paul.

Paul was giving voice to my confusion. But until I wrestled with the fact that he was speaking of himself and not the unwashed heathens, I couldn't follow him to freedom.

Do you see how Paul splits himself into two people? He's trying to explain the *old self*—the walking dead, dominated by sin—and the *new creation*—made alive by Christ and infused with his power. They're both inside us. And if we aren't changing or regenerating or transforming, then the old self will rule the roost. Even when we want to do something nice, the perverseness of our hearts will wreck it.

Here's an example of my walking dead, sinful self. I hear about a friend's good fortune. Maybe her kid won a scholarship. And instantly I wonder, why am I not having this good fortune? It feels unfair. And often, I begrudge that friend. I feel jealous simply because she has something I don't have. This is reality. At any given time, sinful desires or attitudes are coursing through my heart and brain. I don't need to activate it—it's just part of me.

But wait. There's also a new creation in the same soul space. The me with potential. The me God is transforming me into. That person is here too. She's just sort of wimpy because she doesn't get much oxygen.

It's like in Looney Tunes when Bugs Bunny has a mini–Bugs Bunny angel on one shoulder and a mini–Bugs Bunny devil on the other, and each is trying to convince Bugs to follow their advice. The devil always wins.

So I've seen the right path yet persisted in taking the wrong one. Commence the guilt. Wretched indeed. No wonder we stop thinking about why we do what we do. It's depressing to understand the depravity that is our very nature.

But then we turn the page—and BAM!

> Therefore, there is now no condemnation for those who are in Christ Jesus, because through Christ Jesus the law of the Spirit who gives life has set you free from the law of sin and death. For what the law was powerless to do because it was weakened by the flesh, God did by sending his own Son in the likeness of sinful flesh to be a sin offering. And so he condemned sin in the flesh, in order that the righteous requirement of the law might be fully met in us, who do not live according to the flesh but according to the Spirit.
>
> Those who live according to the flesh have their minds set on what the flesh desires; but those who live in accordance with the Spirit have their minds set on what the Spirit desires. The mind governed by the flesh is death, but the mind governed by the Spirit is life and peace. The mind governed by the flesh is hostile to God; it does not submit to God's law, nor can it do so. Those who are in the realm of the flesh cannot please God.
>
> You, however, are not in the realm of the flesh but are in the realm of the Spirit, if indeed the Spirit of God lives in you. And if anyone does not have the Spirit of Christ, they do not belong to Christ. But if Christ is in you, then even though your body is subject to death because of sin, the Spirit gives life because of righteousness. And if the Spirit of him who raised Jesus from the dead is living in you, he

> who raised Christ from the dead will also give life to your mortal bodies because of his Spirit who lives in you.
>
> Therefore, brothers and sisters, we have an obligation—but it is not to the flesh, to live according to it. For if you live according to the flesh, you will die; but if by the Spirit you put to death the misdeeds of the body, you will live.
>
> For those who are led by the Spirit of God are the children of God. (Romans 8:1–14)

Ring, ring. Hello, your Apostleship? Could you please say *one* thing at a time? When you say three things at once, it makes my brain hurt.

But all of the work it takes to really understand Romans 8 is worth it. It's solid protein. Here, Paul is saying the deal is legit. When we trust Jesus for our salvation, we're given a new life. And when God sees us, he sees this new creation. Legally, we're cleared in the books. The requirement is fully met. And now that we're new creations, we're focused on Christ, and we live according to the Spirit.

I know what you're thinking: "Good night, Apostle Paul."

Really. How can we be stamped "approve" yet still wrestle with sin?

First, let's agree that after we give our lives to Christ, we're not autonomous. Our minds are governed by the Spirit. Second, there's clear evidence that only transformation is proof of *right with God*. It's impossible to please him any other way.

Good Christian, are you listening? Life in the Spirit is the *only* way to please God. I'm fidgeting uncomfortably even as I type.

So what about today, like in the real world? A trip to the dentist with a toddler and a faulty muffler. Paul says sin is still a thing. We continue to live in a broken world filled with pain and suffering, and everything that causes pain and suffering. We still have human will and a human body. We will, most likely, die. And we groan and drink our coffee, waiting for the world to be made right.

In Galatians Paul exhorts, "It is for freedom that Christ has set us free. Stand firm, then, and do not let yourselves be burdened again by a yoke of slavery"(Galatians 5:1). A war rages in me between my sinful old nature and the spiritual new creation. There's a process going on. The Spirit will help me as I run after God. More and more of the territory of my heart and mind will be dominated by the ways of Jesus. And slowly, the struggle to *do right* will lessen. There's no devil or angel sitting on my shoulder—there's only me. And as a new creation, I will only think one way. His way. It's the only reasonable option.

And *that* is the gap I found—the gap between chapters 7 and 8.

I saw myself fully reflected in the agonizing words of Romans 7. And I believed all that Romans 8 promised. But I didn't know how to jump from Romans Seven Land to Romans Eight. I didn't know how to live a life governed by the Spirit. I didn't even know what *governed by the Spirit* meant. I thought becoming a Christian meant I was automatically governed by the Spirit. Like, once I got the ticket, I was stamped *New Creation*.

The answer is amazingly complicated. In the legal sense, I'm a new creation. In the process sense—in the percentage of heart ownership, or how much of my life's territory is ruled by God—I'm weak tea, baby. Weak tea.

No wonder all those verses didn't ring true. I didn't understand. My paradigm was built on passive grace. My glasses couldn't *see* governed by the Spirit. So my faith defaulted into behavior modification. And I wasn't so great at that behavior modification stuff. I couldn't even get my socks to match.

I approached my teachers, my mentors, and my pastors with this problem. How do you get to the point where you want to do the selfless thing or pray or read the Bible without making yourself read the Bible? I could force myself to do it but not for long. I wanted to desire God. But I never desired him like I desired pizza. Or *People* magazine.

Those were honest questions directed to good people with sincere hearts. And the answer always came in the form of a question. Always.

"Are you having a regular Quiet Time?"

Bless. It.

Regular Quiet Time. Apparently, that's what *really* separates the sheep from the goats, people. When I prayed for our football team to win the playoffs, I believed my prayers weren't effective. If I couldn't discipline myself to pray when I didn't need something, I figured God wouldn't answer when I did need something. Awesome logic.

When I was a little girl, I'd beg to be sent to Camp Timberlake every summer. Bible camp was the only way to beat the Nebraskan summer doldrums. Best I could figure, there were two kinds of girls at Camp Timberlake. The good girls and the rest of us. The good girls didn't blurt out answers or eat dessert first. They made their beds before they were told to make their beds. Their clothes didn't even get dirty. How I admired them. In my crazy, chaotic mind, I wanted to be peaceful. These girls didn't appear to have much internal struggle going on, so I would try very hard to learn the good girls' ways at camp.

One particularly good girl was named Helen. Helen was simply serene. All the counselors adored her, and she was legitimately kind to everyone. One time I ran back to our cabin to get my beach towel. Careening around a corner, I discovered Helen sitting alone on a bench with her Bible. She was highlighting something in pink. But it was free time. She could've been swimming.

I stood there, blinking in the sun. Helen paused mid-highlight and smiled up at me.

"Don't you want to go swimming?" I stammered, noticing that she was highlighting verses that had been previously underlined.

"Oh, I do. I just need a few more minutes to finish up my Quiet Time."

And there on the path between the cabin and the lake, I realized I couldn't do it. I couldn't jump the crevasse between who I was and who I wanted to be. It was just too far. If I had a million and one opportunities to choose Quiet Time over swimming, swimming would win every single time.

When I asked my elders about my lack of experiencing the power and joy God talks about, I was told to have a regular Quiet Time. The answer was technically appropriate. Obviously, spending time consistently with God is a necessary foundation for any genuine intimacy. This makes perfect sense. In retrospect, I hear differently. Those people were encouraging me to get to know God.

But I didn't hear that then. My passive-grace-paradigm-ears heard, "If you want to learn to desire God, make yourself do it." But because I wasn't tapped into God's strength, I was trying to do spiritual things with physical energy. And *that* was the sticking point. Doing spiritual things with physical energy.

Exhausting.

I wanted to swim, so I did. But as I dove into the cool, green lake water, I knew something wasn't right. Deep inside my heart, I tasted disappointment. I knew I could never make myself into Helen. Helen was on the same trail as Hudson Taylor, even though we were just kids. But something made her want to read the Bible during free time. And that seemed like a little too much for me.

There is some significant irony here. Because my evangelical denomination was so fearful of teaching faith by works, salvation was presented equivalent to justification. In fact, we learned the mnemonic *just as if I'd never sinned* to help us remember *justification* is by grace and nothing else. I missed the part about placing my allegiance with Christ and moving forward with the conviction that Jesus was the One. Understanding that my life was not my own, but rather, it belonged to God. So I kept muddling up the green page with a church life that focused a lot on behavior modification, which feels a lot like—you guessed it—*works*.

I slipped into a life of works because I was avoiding works. I just laughed heartily out loud, a clear indicator that I need to get out more. But here we can see how losing our life to Christ is the only way to gain it. We're dead ducks anywhere else.

All my years growing up—and also in college, marriage, parenting—I could never manage that regular Quiet Time thing. So when problems arose and crises came, or when I examined the gap between Seven and Eight, I felt that I hadn't earned God's ear. I thought the reason I couldn't feel supernatural joy or strength or patience was that lack of Quiet Time. And this belief led to feelings of guilt. Those were hardly warm, fuzzy thoughts, and they only increased my need to move fast and be shallow. Keep working. Keep serving. And I felt some relief in serving. It felt better working for the kingdom of God and away from the kingdom of me.

All of my guilt confirmed that I was stuck in Romans Seven. Over in Eight, there was no condemnation. Over there, they were more than conquerors. It was like living in an apartment building with neighbors who liked to party. I could hear the music and see the lights. I wanted Eight—Dance Nation was going on over there—and Eight was promised to me. But how could I jump the gap?

I asked God for help, and he graciously led me to Dallas Willard. I started investigating all my biblical heroes. I smothered myself with Joseph, Gideon, and Elijah over and over. And then Ruth, David, Peter, and Paul. Over and over. Of course, the teaching of Jesus was omnipresent like a light bulb above it all. But I was specifically inspecting fellow Christ-followers. I needed some answers.

I searched for the *clavis aurea* of discipleship. The golden key. The mysterious thing that, once understood, explained all other mysterious things. How do you live in response to grace rather than attempting to *earn* it?

I loved the stories in the Bible about Gid, Dave, Joe, Eli, and Pete. Those guys were epic failures. Dishonesty, arrogance, depression, doubt, adultery, murder. Not to mention the frequent self-serving temper tantrums. And God loved them so. God's love for these broken servants would lift up off the page and encircle me. Here with this parade of losers, I found hope. It was the love of God that brought hope. He loves them, and he loves me. The clavis aurea wasn't going to be found in behavior. The golden key to understanding our spiritual life can't be located in what we physically do, otherwise David would be voted off the island immediately. No offense, Dave.

Night after night, I'd escape into the stories I thought I knew so well, refusing to leave until I saw what I was missing. I stooped with Gideon in the darkness of a broken vineyard. We were hiding from an invading horde that had stripped the land and burned it bare. His hands are grinding grain between dirty stones. He is terrified and exhausted.

And when God walks in the door, I hear him speak to Gideon's back. God's words to a cowardly, dirty sinner: "Behold, mighty warrior!"

I catch my breath. Because Gideon is real . . . and real angry. He has a bone to pick with God.

"Excuse me? Are you talking to me? With all due respect, where have you been? I'm tired of hearing about what you did in the past. Blah, blah. This is *now*. And it's been seven years of fear. Seven years of loss. I gave up on you because seven years is a long time. You abandoned us."

It's a raw moment. Perhaps this is why God picked Gideon. There's nothing fake about the guy. This is an honest cry from a broken heart.

Then I witness how God lovingly responds. How he cares. God moves toward Gideon, and he answers, "Go in the strength that you have. Am I not sending you?" There's no condemnation. No history lesson. Just God with his arms wide open, saying, "Gideon, you have what you need. You have *me*."

And Gideon is so weak. He needs help believing. He runs around fluffing pillows and making coffee, while God—the Creator of the universe, the great *I AM*—sits in the parlor and waits. Because he loves Gideon. Oh, how he loves him.

I read this story over and over like a thirsty person in the desert. The nation of Israel needed victory over Midian, but Gideon needed God. Gideon was saved when he put his confidence in God. It was a process, but God helped. He turned; he waited. And God was all Gideon needed.

I wanted to speak to God like Gideon spoke to God—frankly and honestly.

So I told God the truth.

"I can't possibly have a regular Quiet Time. I've tried again and again, and I've completely failed at it, along with so many other things I'm supposed to want to do. I feel plastic and hollow. I'm confused at church. Church brings out my smallness and pettiness, but being small and petty is more enjoyable than feeling guilty and bored. I care about you, God, but not like I care about the opinions of people. I want people to like and respect me. I want that more than I've ever wanted you. I don't know why, other than I'm a complete schmuck. I'm afraid of living like Hudson Taylor. I don't want pain or cancer or anything that threatens my family and my home. I want to be safe. But I'm so very tired, God—too tired to keep going like this. I don't want to be stuck in Romans Seven anymore. Tomorrow I'll probably change my mind and act like we've never talked, but in this moment I want to be the person you see when you look at me. I just don't know how to do it."

And God turned.

In my tiny room, laundry piled all around, God stood with his arms open. There was no history lesson. No PowerPoint presentation to illuminate my failure. And he said, "You have what you need. You have *me*."

There was no to-do list. No workbook or program. Just so much God I could barely breathe. I'd done nothing, and I deserved nothing. Romans Eight was here and now.

And suddenly, I *wanted* God. Like a fire burning up wood, I wanted more of this moment. God loved me. It was profound. And I wanted to know him. Deep inside, my old self shuddered and groaned, and the new creation became a speck—tiny but present—on my internal map.

Behold, the kingdom of heaven is at hand.

My faith was weak, and I had little confidence this would last through tomorrow. But I saw Gideon smile back at me from the pages of Scripture. God—the Almighty One who formed the earth and everything in it—stood by my laundry pile. He would help me because he loved me.

And slowly I lifted a different lens to my eye—the same lens given to Gideon, Mrs. Gowan, and Helen—and I stood, blinking in the all-consuming radiance of his love.

And I could *see*.

CHAPTER 5

Birth of an Ezer

It is a law of spiritual life that every act of trust makes the next act less difficult. Trusting becomes like breathing, the natural unconsciousness of the redeemed soul.

—Hannah Whitall Smith, *The Christian's Secret of a Happy Life*

SAY WHAT YOU WILL, BUT SOME THINGS IN THE WORLD NEED to stay regular. Because when it's not regular, life is uncomfortable.

I found myself in the grocery store one morning searching for prunes. My pride prevented me from asking for assistance, as everyone working in the produce section was approximately twelve, and I simply wasn't going to ask a youngster for the location of prunes.

Finally, I found them. Part of the difficulty in locating them is that this particular grocery store no longer called them prunes. They were labeled *sun-dried plums*. In fact, most grocery stores no longer carry prunes, only exotic sounding sun-dried plums.

But a sun-dried plum is clearly still a prune, just with a fancy name change and packaged in a colorful plastic bag.

Apparently, prunes weren't making the grade. Research indicated—yes, this was actually researched—that American women between the ages of twenty-five and fifty-four responded more favorably, and were more likely to purchase, a dried plum over the ubiquitous prune.[6]

6 Jody Ordioni, "Prunes Just Weren't Cool: How Rebranding Can Increase Market Success," July 7, 2016. https://www.brandemix.com/prunes-just-werent-cool-how-rebranding-can-increase-market-success/.

It seems American women associated prunes with aging. Perhaps because there are nutritional and medicinal benefits of prunes that we need as we progress through life. Or perhaps because a plum shrivels up into a prune, sort of like the lady who lounged poolside for the entire Clinton administration. But the prevailing thinking was that only the elderly needed prunes. Jane Shopper's inner dialogue went like this: "I am not old, and my goal is never to *be* old, so I will not pay $1.99 for a bag of reality. Thank you very much."

However, it turns out that Jane was willing to pay $2.99 for a brightly colored bag of sun-dried plums.

Interestingly, the research also indicated that women outside of America were completely fine with calling a prune a prune. Hmm.

Basically, the prune is a beneficiary of *rebranding*. Rebranding is the process of giving a product or service a new name or representation. A package may be changed or a logo streamlined, but the essence remains the same. Marketers do this with the goal of adjusting people's perceptions. Almost always, they're trying to change a negative perception into a more positive one.

A recent rebranding success story involved deodorant. My son came to me one day and said, "Mom, I want this new deodorant. It's cool, and I like it." Thrilled that my teenager was pursuing hygiene, I asked him what this new deodorant was called.

"Old Spice."

Was he kidding? Old Spice, as in the company that produced potent aftershave, a Christmastime favorite of grandfathers since its invention?

Turns out Old Spice had rebranded. It was now cool. It promised to make you "smell like a man." Having grown up with all brothers, I would personally never have chosen this slogan. Isn't the whole purpose of deodorant to *not* smell like a man? But Old Spice currently claims a whopping percentage of the teenage male deodorant market, effectively disproving my business savvy. These kids will be buying deodorant for the next sixty years, or at least until they switch to the aforementioned aftershave.

Rebranding done right is powerful. And apparently, lucrative.

Rebranding is also used to make familiar things fresh. This happens all the time in the hospital where I work. In an effort to compel busy people to stop and listen when a code is called on the overhead paging system, they frequently change the code words. For example, *Code Five* once meant someone in the hospital was becoming dangerously aggressive—a very important piece of information to understand and respond to with appropriate action. But worker bees are busy, and there's always so much noise. When the code suddenly changed to *Code Alpha*, everyone wondered what it meant, even though we'd received seventeen emails and six trainings on the matter. The intercom announced, "Code Alpha, floor eight," and we all paused, wondering aloud, "What's 'Code Alpha'?" And the folks on the eighth floor looked down at their badges, clearly labeled with the new codes, and then responded.

The administrators had relabeled—or rebranded—the codes so that we could hear them again.

Of course, it's possible to rebrand badly. In the face of perpetually declining market share, Radio Shack rebranded as The Shack. Don't remember that happening? Exactly. The Shack went out of business a few years later. Likewise, if the hospital changes codes too frequently, all the workers become confused and grumpy. It's a delicate balance creating just enough change to keep people listening but not so much that they can't keep up.

Why am I blathering on about this? Well, changing the name for things was colossally helpful for me with this paradigm-shifting business. After years of failing at discipleship and Quiet Time, I needed a change.

Perhaps there are people that I've horribly offended by rejecting the words *Quiet Time*. I do apologize.

For the record, there are many good QT resources out there, and there's absolutely nothing wrong with the words *quiet* or *time*. Spending time alone with God on a regular basis in an effort to get to know him better is essential. But the phrase *Quiet Time* sort of settled in my psyche upon piles of guilt and failure. Quiet Time represented all my lackluster attempts to change my behavior so that I could line up with God's will.

Once I understood that only pursuing God would change my behavior, I needed lots of help to stay on course. My new patterns looked like Bambi wobbling into the meadow.

And then Dallas Willard said something like this: "One must train as well as try."[7]

Hmm. When you go to the hospital for emergency surgery, would you prefer your physician to have spent his years in school *trying* to take out an appendix or *training* to take out an appendix?

Exactly.

From the time I was a little peep, I tried to behave like I thought God wanted me to behave. Sometimes I tried extra hard. I'd fill in the blanks, write in the margins, and even use the concordance to find parallel verses. I know—so good, right? But then I'd get tired and frustrated, and I'd quit.

To stay sane, I developed a low effort trying system. I used things outside myself to make me behave. Church attendance, Bible study, volunteering in the Little Lamb room. I tuned in to Christian radio and listened to the one-minute sermons occasionally played between songs. I kept my oar in, so to speak. I lived in a God culture—as compared to the heathens at the gym—and kept external reminders of my identity. Like my pretty pink coffee mug with a Bible verse on the side. These reminders were like ants at a picnic: present but not impactful. I was aware of the presence of God, but his presence didn't impact my command of the situation, whatever the situation might be.

So I seized the word *training* and threw out *discipleship*. Not because the concepts were different, but because I needed a new word to hear. This rebranding brought something that was absolutely essential to my transformation—hope. When I heard the word *training*,

7 Dallas Willard, *The Spirit of the Disciplines: Understanding How God Changes Lives* (Grand Rapids, MI: Family Christian Press, 2001), 98.

I felt something different. I was slightly less pessimistic. It wasn't about trying to *do* something different; it was about training to *be* different.

Around this time, I was living inside the book of Ruth. Just like with Gideon, this story grabbed hold of my heart and wouldn't let go. I read it over and over, sometimes twenty times in one sitting. I was in Ruth so long, I had to pitch a tent and join her and Naomi on the fringe of existence. While tramping back and forth between Moab and Bethlehem, I accidentally found *The Gospel of Ruth* by Carolyn Custis James on my bookshelf. I have no idea how it got there. Possibly someone gave it to me when I wasn't paying attention. Apparently, I need a lot of improvement because I get unsolicited books all the time. And there I was, gleaning grain every night with my girl Ruth, when *wham*! A book completely dedicated to the subject landed on my shelf.

And I read it. Without putting it down.

It devastated me in all the right ways.

Here's what moved my world: *ezer*. One little word with which I was unfamiliar. Ezer is God's word for "woman." It's Hebrew for "strength." In Genesis, God called Eve *ezer kenegdo*, which translates to "strength corresponding to him." God used the word *ezer* to refer to himself many times in the Old Testament, as his strength frequently came to Israel's aid. It's a military term: "We wait in hope for the Lord; he is our help and our shield [ezer]" (Psalm 33:20).

Carolyn Custis James goes on to rebrand Eve:

> Putting the facts together, isn't it obvious that the ezer is a warrior? And don't we already know this in our bones? God created His daughters to be ezer-warriors with our brothers. He deploys the ezer to break the man's loneliness by soldiering with him wholeheartedly and at full strength for God's gracious kingdom.[8]

8 Carolyn Custis James, "The Ezer-Kenegdo: Ezer Unleashed," FaithGateway, March 20, 2015, https://www.faithgateway.com/ezer-unleashed/.

Talk about a paradigm shift. It's difficult to overstate how much *this*—the understanding that I am an ezer-warrior—has impacted my worldview.

Night after night, I'd slug it out with Ruth. Sweat, risk, work, breathe. This woman is a foreigner who turns a sleepy little town on its ear. She breaks a bunch of rules. Risks her life. Why? Yes, because she loves Naomi, but that's not all. Somewhere in the vile darkness of Moab, living among strange people with stranger ways, Ruth encounters the God who never fails. And Ruth chooses God. She places all of her trust in him.

The family of Elimelech needs an heir. But Ruth needs God. She is saved when she puts her confidence in God, and her allegiance to him makes the rest of the story possible.

Ezer-warrior. My allegiance to God is what makes it possible—whatever *it* is.

And hope grew. I was training for a purpose. I was God's warrior, which was infinitely more interesting than my previous form of doing faith.

To be clear, I take sole responsibility for my becoming a Good Christian. My church, my teachers, and my spiritual mentors were not the cause of my being fake. My refusal to give God my life in its entirety, plus my infantile need to remain as comfortable as possible, were my downfalls.

So now that I identified myself as an ezer-warrior in training, what exactly was I supposed to do when I rolled out of bed? I had no castles to storm or anything. What does warrior training look like?

The immersive Bible reading seemed to be effective, although admittedly a little unsettling. For a girl who rarely made it through a one-page morning devotional, the need to read and reread the same portion of Scripture felt strange. I continued to participate in formal Bible studies but found myself eager to finish filling in those blanks so I could be free to wander around Jericho or Capernaum or wherever my obsession had landed. The formal Bible studies did seem to inspire ideas, like turning on the GPS. Someone mentioned Jonah, and there

I was for weeks. I think it was because I was learning to see with new eyes. I had to stay and *see* before I could move on.

Recently, I watched a video where colorblind people are given glasses to help them perceive a fuller range of color. Most of the people shouted or swore or danced. One man grabbed his daughter's face in his hands and burst into tears, saying, "Your eyes are so blue they make me cry." Naturally, this made *me* cry.

I was experiencing something similar. With a shifted paradigm, I began seeing many things that simply weren't visible before. Unlike the passive flannelgraph version of Bible stories, many of the biblical characters were loud, rude, and demanding.

For example, Bartimaeus. The dude won't stop yelling. He disturbs and embarrasses the very people he depends on for the handouts keeping him alive. And Jesus stops to ask the blind beggar, "What do you want me to do for you?" Bartimaeus answers with profound simplicity, "Rabbi, I want to see."

Why had I never noticed this before? Bartimaeus cuts loose from his safety net. He has no plan B. He makes himself unpopular with the crowd that literally feeds him, and his fevered shouting interrupts the parade of important people following Jesus through the gates. Bart makes his community look a little dicey. The city elders are probably thinking, "People are going to wonder why we can't control our beggars."

But Bart is just getting started.

When he jumps up to go to Jesus, Bartimaeus throws away his cloak. As a blind person, wouldn't you want to hang on to that? I work with people who are visually impaired. They are never cavalier about where they leave things. Clearly, Bart does not plan on coming back blind. His every hope is in Jesus.

Bartimaeus, the patient, needs eyes that could see. Bartimaeus, the man, needs God. Bart is saved when he places all of his confidence in Christ. Jesus confirms it, saying, "Go. Your faith has healed you." But note how the story ends. Bartimaeus can finally see. He has a million and one things he could do—find his friends, embrace his family, sign a book deal—but that's not what he does. Bart follows Jesus.

Wow.

Gideon trusted God—and took bigger and bigger risks—until God helped him to defeat an army the size of Canada using horns and flashlights. Ruth adopted God—and took bigger and bigger risks—until she sacrificed all her hard-won safety to rescue Naomi's dead. Bartimaeus risked his status quo for the life Jesus offered, and in the face of overwhelming love, he didn't focus on the gift. He focused on the Giver.

Inside these stories I could see some new things. First, there appeared to be an equation. Confidence + risk = more confidence. That was helpful. Second, it seemed everyone was supposed to move forward in the strength that they had. And they all seemed fairly broken to start. Gideon was angry and bitter, with zero social clout. Ruth was a foreigner and a woman, with zero social clout. Bartimaeus was blind and penniless, with zero social clout.

Clearly, God wasn't concerned about the résumé when he set out to hire. After all, the outward skill set—or lack of a skill set—can be so misleading. God looks inside the soul and sees the heart of a warrior. A formative definition of warrior appeared to be "willingness to risk what has been received from God in order to receive more from God."

Well, that sounds completely intimidating, mostly because I've built my life around being safe and comfortable.

So there I was, just trying to let all that sink in. You know, the planning phase of my training. I was going to plan for a while, preferably a long while.

And then I walked into the parable of the talents, which of course read completely differently with my new glasses on.

Night after night I would crowd up close to Jesus, squeezing right between Peter and John. And the Rabbi speaks.

Jesus tells a story about a boss who leaves his employees in charge of varying amounts of the company. The man put in charge of a large percentage of the company ends up doubling the assets of his department. The guy given a medium amount also works hard, and he doubles the assets of his department. But the dude given just a little bit doesn't want to risk anything because the boss is a tough man—aggressive in business, to put it mildly. Little Bit thinks, "Better hold on to what I have so that I'm safe. When the boss gets back, I'll just turn this back over to him."

The boss eventually returns from vacay and calls a staff meeting to go over the accounts of the company. Each employee has to pony up. The first and second employees are able to report that business is good. Doubled, in fact. The boss is thrilled. He praises them for their hard work and loyalty and promotes them both. He announces, "Welcome to the joy of the master," which I think must be a company bonus plan.

But then Little Bit gets up. He reminds the boss of his harsh reputation in the industry. Little Bit describes his strategy to retain the assets: "I hid in the coffee room the whole time you were gone. I was afraid I might lose money for you, so I did nothing." Needless to say, the boss is irate. He shouts, "If you *knew* I was obsessed with profits, why wouldn't you try to make profits? You idiot. I'm giving your department to the first guy and throwing you out of the company. Don't bother trying to collect unemployment!"

In the story circle at Jesus's feet, I want to poke Pete and John. Guys, ask questions. How is this fair? Because the last guy—Little Bit—is me. His plan seems reasonable. I mean, it's not a *great* plan, but it makes some sense.

My new glasses indicated that it was not only important to risk but—gulp—it was commanded.

Ring, ring. Hello, God? Umm, I need some further explanation. First, I've been confused for years because I thought *talents* referred to, you know, singing or painting or something. I thought it was about using my gifts for your kingdom. And honestly, I thought I was doing that. Didn't you see? I volunteered, I led, I created for your kingdom. And that last VBS—the one with the craft involving feathers—surely counts for double.

No response other than an overwhelming compulsion to read the parable of the talents again and again. So I did.

Ring, ring. I'm really trying to get this, God. Who is the boss of the company? Is that you? Why is the boss so mean? What about your love? Why would you take away the little bit that Little Bit had? Why throw him out? Where is grace? I'm confused. Why on earth didn't Peter ask questions? I don't think he got this either, God. I think he faked it.

More reading and research. It was slow going. And every night I'd squish back into the story circle at Jesus's feet.

Ring, ring. Okay, it was a company. The servants were employed by the master, and when they took the job, they agreed to work. They were on the clock. Doing nothing wasn't an option while they were serving the company. I think I can see why Little Bit was fired for hiding in the coffee room. But what are the talents? If the talents are the resources of the master, then what are the talents in my life? My spiritual gifts or *everything*? I don't know how to multiply everything.

I went back to Gideon and Ruth. I watched Bart spend his newly received fortune on following Jesus. I prayed a simple prayer. *Rabbi, I want to see.*

Suddenly, I heard my God phone ringing in my head.

Ring, ring. Ring, ring. Ring, ring. I hesitated. My breathing became ragged as I answered.

Hello?

It was God, and he wanted to talk. And for perhaps the first time in my life, I was attentively listening with every cell in my body.

"I love how you name things."

My heart flooded with insane joy. I wanted to get up and do cartwheels, except I was supposed to be paying attention, and I hadn't done a cartwheel in about three decades.

"My grace makes your employment in the company possible. Little Bit took the job but didn't take the grace."

I knew it. I knew grace was there! Grace makes the whole company run. So what is the talent, God? What *is* the talent?

"Your status inside my kingdom."

Huh?

"Gideon took the courage he had and risked it all for more courage. Ruth took the safety she had and risked it all for more safety. Bartimaeus took the gift he was given and cashed it in the right place."

So I'm supposed to take what I have from you and risk it for more? More what?

"More faith, power, and peace. More of me. Salvation is a life. Weren't you listening in the story circle?"

And I got it. The only safe place is with *him*. Everything I've ever wanted is all here inside him. It's always been here, like the backside of the mirror, but now I could see it. And I felt something incredible, like wanting to run and sit still at the same time. Like watching a thousand happy endings all at once. The hero always wins. The bad guy is completely vanquished. Peace rules the land. Whatever happens, we're victorious. Whatever happens, we're more than conquerors.

"Welcome to the joy of the Master."

I became aware of my own deep breaths. I was sitting in my Hello Kitty pajamas on the middle of my bed. I wondered what on earth just happened. And I said out loud to myself, "That was nothing on *earth*, honey. That was the kingdom of God."

Breathe in, breathe out. Heart rate beginning to normalize.

Well, that does it. I'm in. With all the conviction I had to offer, I locked the door to the coffee room. Doing nothing would never be an option again.

Somewhere in the darkness sounded the slap of skin on skin, and the wail of a little baby girl filled the night—the birth of an ezer.

I'd like to say that it was mostly an upward trajectory from there. That I grew strong and courageous and, with God as my guide, went forth to subdue my territory. But seriously, if you're still reading, you know me better. Bumpy road ahead. Bumpy road.

However, serious traction was gained that night. Warrior training wasn't like anything I'd ever done before. And I loved it even though it felt crazy weird, because it made way more sense than anything I'd ever experienced.

So far, warrior training involved taking what I had and risking it for more. Without risk, I couldn't move forward, which explained why I couldn't move forward with my previously frustrating, on-again, off-again Quiet Time. It didn't involve risking anything. Instead of keeping myself safe, I had to look for opportunities to risk.

So immediately, I included this prayer at the end of my total-immersion reading sessions: "Show me what you want me to risk."

Because I truly didn't know, and I still had wobbly Bambi legs.

For sure I wasn't just risking to risk. That's silly. If I saw myself as an employee, not my own boss, I had to use the master's resources to increase the company. Okay, sounds like a plan. And then I got out of bed and started my day. I think I made it halfway down the stairs before Romans Seven slapped me in the face. *Gah.*

It would be way easier to do all this stuff if the world wasn't populated with so many people. Or social media hadn't been invented. Or my husband had just loaded the dishwasher from back to front.

I heard Gideon laughing. Apparently, this warrior hadn't figured out the concept of starting small.

I wobbled onward.

CHAPTER 6

Hoarders and Ninjago

"I don't think . . ."
"Then you shouldn't talk," said the Hatter.
—Lewis Carroll, *Alice in Wonderland*

WE DON'T HAVE CABLE. MY HUSBAND SAYS WE CAN'T AFFORD it, but secretly I'm pretty sure it's a boundary, like a baby gate at the top of the stairs.

If we had cable, I might never leave the couch. Watching obscene amounts of television is one of my innate talents. Very few people appreciate that watching twelve straight hours of entertainment is a serious accomplishment.

The greatest thing about not having cable is that when we go on vacations, we always stay somewhere that *does* have cable. Like 323 channels. Sweet mother of pearl, *now* we're talking.

One time, we were staying with my folks so my children could visit their grandparents and I could visit their television. My dad had over 600 channels. Clearly, the talent is in the genes. My husband missed me and came to the couch to spend some time with me.

"What do you want to watch?" I asked. I totally understand romance. And he responded with the right answer: "Anything."

And that is when I stumbled upon the most horrifically voyeuristic peep show delving into the brokenness of the human soul. It's a program called *Hoarders*. In this show, a family has requested professional help because a loved one has a form of mental illness called obsessive hoarding. Something has gone awry in their neuromatter, and the *out* switch is broken. This means that material possessions come into the house, but nothing goes out. Nothing. Often the show kicks off with some sort of crisis. The homeowner may be threatened with eviction, or perhaps they're in danger of losing custody of a minor due to unsafe living conditions.

This isn't an individual who simply likes to keep things. This is brokenness. This is a sickness of human nature on display. Over the years, the house has filled up. Rooms are forgotten. The homeowner reports they haven't been able to get to the back bedroom since 1987. The possessions have become the possessor, and reason has fled the premises. The only thing left to this victim is the pile of refuse. Anything valuable or lovely was long ago corrupted or lost by the sheer volume of stuff.

Sitting in my parents' overly air-conditioned basement, we watched a life that had warped into death without the person even knowing. I had never seen the show, and naturally, I expected something positive to happen before it wrapped. Surely, we were watching all of this because the poor soul was going to get the help they needed. Serious help. In a few minutes, the tide would turn and this individual would start the long road back to sanity.

But it didn't happen. For fifty minutes we walked through a macabre death scene, and ultimately, the victim chose to remain with her poison. The psychologist, the professional organizer, and the cleaning crew slowly loaded everything back into their industrial-style vans. The cameraman kept rolling, and the parting image was of a real-life zombie turning her back to her only source of help. As the credits roll, the zombie closes the door of her home, sealing her crypt.

My husband felt nauseated. He doesn't have the viewership muscles I've acquired.

But later that night, I thought about that woman. Buried alive in her possessions.

In addition to wrestling with the very real issue of entertainment versus exploitation, I was left with a powerful question: How does a human being arrive at the point of complete self-enslavement? There was an obvious concluding thought to these graphic images.

Letting go is important.

And for the ezer, it's critical.

Progress in the warrior department was slow. Although I had a new frame of reference, I had an old set of behaviors and an old way of thinking that flew the plane most of the time. My obsessive reading regime was camping out in Romans. Hard as a rock and uncomfortable for pitching a tent. There aren't a lot of narratives in Romans. It's all solid. The apostle Paul has a gift for the run-on sentence—*please* take a breath, your Apostleship—and I was hammering it out one verse at a time. Case in point, Romans 12.

> Therefore, I urge you, brothers and sisters, in view of God's mercy, to offer your bodies as a living sacrifice, holy and pleasing to God—this is your true and proper worship. Do not conform to the pattern of this world, but be transformed by the renewing of your mind. Then you will be able to test and approve what God's will is—his good, pleasing and perfect will. (Romans 12:1–2)

There was a lot going on here, and my warrior senses were tingling. Paul talks about patterns. There's a pattern of the world, and we are conformed to it. Warrior training involves busting out of the pattern so that our minds can be reprogrammed. The old program must be shut down so the new software can take over. With the new software running, I can risk more of what God has given me to further my efforts to double the assets in my part of the company.

Okay. So what I heard Paul say is that my Romans Seven Self isn't fully aware of my sin habits and is blind to the ways of the warrior. It can't recognize God's will, and it's totally content with that. I could be a Good Christian for the next sixty years, and my old sin nature would continue to tell me I'm on the right path.

Well, that's terrifying.

It's disturbing how any true meditation on Scripture leads to a greater understanding of how I have completely accepted my life as a miscreant.

And in this befuddled state, I grew up a little bit. For years, I operated with the understanding that my Romans Seven Self—the old creation—was obsessed with overt badness. Like when I was an angry jerk or when I gossiped or when I backdated reports.

Turns out it was also me driving Wednesday carpool. Or me shopping or helping my kids with homework. My Romans Seven Self was just me being me. The old creation was my baseline.

But wait. Where is my Romans Eight Self? The *new* creation?

Largely undeveloped. Sitting on the bench.

My Romans Eight Self existed, but mostly in the form of untapped potential. Years ago, there was a lovely little forest right next to my home. One day, a construction company cleared the land, leaving a large pile of dirt and a sign that read "Future Site of the Hampton Inn." But then the economy tanked. Apparently, money was tied up elsewhere, and the lot was occupied by nothing but weeds for the next six years. The vacant lot was a designated patch of untapped potential.

So if you spread out a map of my soul that showed the territory under the control of my Romans Seven Self and the territory under the control of my Romans Eight Self, what would the percentages be?

I struggled with this question. A lot. I quickly called a staff meeting of the psyche. It was time to read the spreadsheet. I went through the different departments.

Did I trust God with my kids? If they were taken away from me tomorrow, would I be able to stand and say, "It is well with my soul"?

The answer was no.

Did I trust God with my marriage? If Mike told me he didn't love me or want to live with me anymore, would I be able to stand and say, "It is well with my soul"?

The answer was no.

Well, what about my career? If my boss fired me, would I be able to stand and say, "It is well with my soul"?

The answer was no.

Was there *any* part of me that belonged completely to God? Any part that wasn't under the control of my own will?

The answer was no.

I'm not one to keep my opinions to myself, so I pushed back.

That's entirely unfair, God. Everyone wants to keep what they love. Everyone recoils and flees from pain. What you're asking is unreasonable.

And this is the plight of the Romans Seven Self. Unreasonable allegiance was tough to swallow. I knew it, God. I knew all of this would lead to Hudson Taylor. I don't want to go there. I don't want to trust you in the midst of pain. I don't want to watch my children suffer if heaven fails to answer my prayers. No thanks.

What I did want was to do was throw my Bible at the wall. But I simply had too much Good Christian in me to do it. So I slammed it shut and stomped out. Believe it or not, Apostle Paul, some of us have a life to live. Kids to feed and bills to pay. We can't just sit around all day writing impossible stuff on paper. But as I headed out of the room, I looked back and saw Gideon. And Ruth. My friends. Reaching out with stories that said, "We've been right where you are. Don't give up."

So once again, I banged right up against the need to be my own god. I was grumpy about this for a few weeks.

But I couldn't forget the night God called me on the phone in my head. I couldn't act like it never happened. There was way too much God in that moment to simply write it off.

What if I tried using the God phone again? Apparently, I had rebranded prayer into talking on the phone with God. Let's pause for a moment and listen to the sound of church fathers rolling in their graves. But for me, it was vastly easier to talk on the phone than to pray.

Ring, ring. Hello, God? I'm stuck. I really don't know how *not* to be my own god. Because at the end of the day, I can risk some parts of me, but I can't risk my kids. Or my husband. I can't, and more importantly, I don't want to. So you see, I'm stuck.

Silence on the line.

God? Are you there? Please. I don't want to be Hudson Taylor.

And then I heard God speak.

"What do you want from me?"

Wait, why are you asking me? I don't know what I want. Aren't you God? Don't you know what I want? But suddenly, I did know what I wanted. I just wasn't brave enough to say it out loud.

I wanted to stay in control. Essentially, I wanted to be like God. Well, I was too afraid to admit that. But I was definitely proposing some sort of co-leading situation. Like, I would tell God the things that really mattered to me, and he would see my point and respond in an accommodating manner. Because that's what I thought prayer was.

"No. I am God. You are not."

Uh oh. Had I actually—sort of—asked God if he would share his divinity with me? Yes, I had. I asked the Almighty if he might deal me in on the job. Gulp. All of my upbringing told me that some serious smiting was just around the corner.

But the exact opposite was true. I didn't feel condemnation. Throughout my fledgling warrior experiences, I became increasingly aware that honest conversations with God never upset him. More and more I realized that honest conversations were the only way forward. It did no good to act like I was fine when I wasn't. Or that I understood when I didn't. God wanted the honest exchange because he loved *me*, not my Good Christian behavior.

Me.

"Keep reading, my love."

And then I cried. Every time I used the God phone, the conversation ended with me feeling so incredibly adored. It kept me going, which was good because moving forward was going to be rough. It would require the death of my old self, and no matter how you slice the loaf, dying is hard.

That night I went back to Romans. I found Paul still in Corinth.

I'm sorry I slammed my Bible in your face, your Apostleship.

And Paul, with his dimmed eyes and scraggly beard, smiled. Ever the patient professor, he pointed to the page. I read Romans 12. First two verses, again and again.

What does it mean to be a living sacrifice?

Paul smiled wider. Bingo. The next step was to be a living sacrifice.

Here's what I originally thought this verse meant. Focus on the green page *really* hard and strive to be as pure as possible, because sacrificial animals are always innocent. Like, don't binge-watch Netflix. To offer my good and proper worship, I must *do* things that are good and *not do* things that are bad.

And this is why it's so important to get first things first. We must understand that salvation is a life, meaning I now belong to God. I am his child. But I'm also his soldier, his servant, his slave, his employee. All of these titles paint a picture of subordination. Jesus himself modeled this for us when he explained that he is subordinate to the Father: "For I have come down from heaven not to do my will but to do the will of him who sent me" (John 6:38).

Left to my own devices, the green page gets pretty murky. So when I used to read Paul's urging us to offer ourselves as living sacrifices, it felt optional. Perhaps he just strongly suggested we do it. But that thinking only makes sense wearing the old glasses. With the new glasses, I see Paul saying, "Listen up, Buttercup. Just because we serve a merciful God who doesn't drop the sin hammer immediately, don't waste time. Move forward by killing off the Romans Seven Self so that what remains is pleasing to God. This is the only form of tribute he accepts."

So naturally, we ask: How? How do we move forward when we've identified that our Romans Seven Self dominates practically the entire map?

We are subordinate to God, and we must offer ourselves—not optional—in a two-step process. First, we unplug from everything that is *not* God. The paradigms, the gestalts, and the worldviews—everything we've subconsciously formed while watching YouTube and living in our culture—that have programmed our minds. We search for sin patterns or grooves that we live in, and then we try to bust out. Second, we let God fill the emptiness with new programming. This is the essence of being transformed. The old is made into something new. As this happens, we don't simply *try* to do what Jesus would do. We do it.

My dad was fond of saying, "Never try to teach a pig to sing." His children, of course, had no idea what he meant by it. But we guessed that we were somehow the pig and Dad was tired of trying to teach us something.

Recently, I came across the full quote by Lazarus Long, a character in several of Robert Heinlein's novels: "Never try to teach a pig to sing. It wastes your time and it annoys the pig."[9] It basically means pigs weren't made to perform at the Met. If you want an animal that sings, you need a bird.

A light bulb flickered on. The Romans Seven Self would never, ever sing. The pig had to die so the bird could live.

Whoa.

My previous understanding of these verses was that my optional-ish job was to govern myself by trying to do good things as well as by trying not to do bad things. God would feel worshiped when I did good things. Through this process, I would magically stop thinking like the world, and God would create something new inside me that could finally understand his will.

Wow. My old understanding was really lame.

New understanding. I am the lamb. It's me. I have to die. There's no other way forward than to kill off my Romans Seven Self. How do I do this? By surrender. Submission. All of me belongs to God. Because I'm attentive to God, he'll show me the invisible sin grooves inside me and help me break out, one groove at a time. Then God will fill the empty space with a new groove—a God-dominated groove. So instead of worrying all the time about serving myself or serving God, I just get to live. And now I'm free.

---

9 Robert A. Heinlein, *Time Enough for Love: The Lives of Lazarus Long* (New York: Ace Books, New York, 1987), 3.

I heard Ruth and Gideon cheer. Yes. You're getting it. We followed God not because we wanted to be heroic, but because God was the only reasonable way forward.

I pictured the hoarder's house again. Piled high with so much stuff it was literally killing her. I remember the cameraman trying to maneuver his way to the kitchen, and the woman was only concerned that he might upset one of her piles. She couldn't see that it was all garbage. That in holding on too tightly, she had turned her treasure to trash. The woman looked like a prisoner slavishly in love with the bars on her cell. It was ludicrous. The poor woman thought her hoard would keep her safe. She couldn't let go because her reason told her that these things equaled love. The piles of possessions equaled life. Her mind fed her a lie which created the feeling that all the people trying to help her were her attackers.

I remember the pain in her face and the blankness in her eyes. Apparently, she'd agreed to this invasion of her home and her privacy. I'm sure legal papers were signed. On some level she wanted help, but then the rescuers arrived and challenged her reason. The psychologist tried to get her to think differently. But anyone could see it in her face. "I can't let go of what I love. Please don't come here and ask me to do it."

I tried to connect the dots. What about my treasure? My husband, my kids. My wonderfully amazing friends. My career. Perhaps handing them over to God felt unreasonable because my brain was feeding me a lie. And my rescuer felt like an attacker because I couldn't let go. It was a lie to believe that human relationships and material goods could ever give me the safety, wholeness, or satisfaction I so desperately craved. As I clung to them, I became ludicrous. Holding on too tightly would eventually poison my treasure.

What if God is who he says he is? What if he's truly for me and not against me? What if he's working every setback and every success together for ultimate good? What would life be like if I lived as though I believed he was my rescuer? What if I accepted that my reasoning was faulty, and I could just trust him to be God?

Unlike the innocent little lamb, I became fully aware of what the sacrifice had to do. One of my mom's favorite sayings bubbled to the surface of my thoughts. "The problem with living sacrifices is that they keep crawling off the altar."

My Romans Seven Self doesn't want to die. When I feel afraid or unsafe, it's my Romans Seven Self not wanting to let go. When God seems unreasonable, it's my Romans Seven Self fighting back. The pig will never sing. Seven will never understand Eight. But with more and more God grooves in place, this new way of being and thinking becomes more normal.

So how does one kill off the old self? One bite at a time, I suppose, like eating an elephant. There's a lot of discussion in the church about spiritual disciplines. And many things can be labeled a discipline, similar to how the word *exercise* can encompass running a marathon or strolling out to get the mail. I was interested in learning how to get on with the business of being a sacrifice. Specifically, how not to climb down from the altar the second things got hard or people didn't like me or my favorite show came on. Hmm. What to do?

Although I wasn't keen on the idea of engaging in spiritual disciplines—thanks to my perpetual failure with anything involving discipline—I knew I couldn't avoid it altogether. Warrior training would definitely involve development in the area of self-control. But where should I begin? It was like hitting the broad side of a barn. I had a vast storehouse of sinful behaviors, patterns, and thinking. And now I was aware that what I could see was only the tip of the iceberg. Awesome.

Ring, ring. Hello, God? Is there any particular place you would like me to start this journey of mortification?

I didn't have to wait. There was an immediate response.

"Stop talking."

What? Stop talking? What does that mean? How is that a spiritual discipline? I was thinking we'd start with something that would beef up my faith or my ability to trust. You want me to take a vow of silence? I'm a mother. I'm married. I work. I can't go around not talking. People need me to talk.

I heard Gideon laughing again.

I remembered that the way of the warrior was about saying yes to God. Okay, God. But you're gonna have to show me how to do that. Telling the mountain to throw itself into the sea is one thing. Asking a mother not to talk is entirely different.

I pulled out a blank journal. I had a zillion to choose from. In the many attempts to reboot my Quiet Time, I'd frequently treat myself to a new journal. Several of them had approximately one and a half pages filled in. Most were completely pristine. Opening a sparkly notebook covered with flowers, I wrote down all the ways I could stop talking in real life. I was surprised at how many ideas filled up the page.

And then I trained.

Not like those people who post all of their workouts on social media. More like a ship in a hurricane, trying to stay the course. I would read the list in the morning, and then in the evening, I'd try to remember any instances of actually not talking. And I'd write them down.

It was slow going. It was hard not to share my every waking thought because so many of my thoughts are absolutely right. The people I encounter every day are so blessed to have me. Truly. You're welcome, friends.

I noticed that it was hardest to stop talking with my kids. I mean, if they would just listen the first or even the seventh time I said something, my not-talking training would be a breeze. Beside the fact that they were normal children, my son was also going through a Ninjago phase. If you're not familiar with Ninjago, then you are a lucky, lucky person. It's fabulously riveting to preadolescent boys but absolute mumbo jumbo to anyone else. I found that if I couldn't talk *at* my kid, I often wanted to walk away. Like right in the middle of his story. He'd walk behind me and try to finish speaking quickly to the back of my shirt.

I started cluing in on why God picked this as my starting place.

So I forced myself sit down and listen to my son. It felt like poking myself in the eye with a spoon. There were seven main ninjas, and each of them had a dragon. Long strings of incomprehensible dialogue about dragon stuff. And then ninja stuff. I forced myself to wait and listen. Around the twenty-minute mark, I contemplated *actually* poking my eye with a spoon.

But my kid has a pretty awesome smile.

I'd report this small progress back to the sparkly flower journal. I wondered when I would know this spiritual discipline thing was working. To keep myself interested, I visited my friends in the Bible and let them tell me what a good job I was doing. I imagined Paul giving me a smiley face sticker.

My warrior training also included continuing with the obsessive reading marathons. During this time, I was dogging Elijah.

It's a hard place to hang out. Elijah's not a big talker. And he smells like a man. Everywhere we go is extremely hot and dry. There's a famine ravaging the land. The skin-and-bone livestock bawl for water. Their moaning slowly ebbs away until the flies come to claim them. Life disappears completely from the landscape. It is brutal. But I know Mount Carmel is on the horizon. I want to encourage the people. God is coming to your rescue. But all they can see is desolation.

Finally, the day arrives, and we trudge up the mountain. I'm surprised that the people followed, given their state of exhaustion. No one speaks. It takes too much energy. Their faces are drawn and gaunt. By the time we reach the top, the prophets of Baal are already there. I stand among the crowd, squinting into the morning sun.

Tension fills the air. This isn't the showdown I expected. I thought it would feel like a football game. Or maybe a WWE slap down. But there's no excitement. This is the atmosphere of a courtroom or an execution. As we stand in the silence, all I hear is the blazing wind blowing up the side of the mountain. It's painfully hot and dry. One spark would be more than enough to start a fire.

Elijah shouts, "'How long will you waver between two opinions? If the Lord is God, follow him; but if Baal is God, follow him'" (1 Kings 18:21).

The crowd says nothing.

I look at the parched children of God, suddenly understanding so much more. God's people were Good Christians before Good Christian was a thing. I want to cry out, "The only safe place is with God! I just learned it too."

But then the prophets of Baal fill our ears with hysterical singing and chanting. The crowd shifts indifferently on their feet. They look between Elijah and the giant swarm of prophets—no allegiance to either. It becomes clear that hope itself is on trial. These people will worship a stick of butter if it brings the rain.

The prophets get nowhere with their rituals. They faint from blood loss and heat exhaustion. Finally, Elijah calls the people to him. We circle around while he carefully rebuilds the altar. Twelve stones.

Do you see it? It's Israel. God's people. This is a message for all who belong to God. I want to cry out, but my tongue withers in the heat.

And then the crowd stirs uneasily as they watch Elijah dig a trench around the altar. This isn't customary. Suddenly, we're paying full attention.

Elijah's robe whips in the scorching heat. He commands that four water jugs be brought to the altar. The crowd presses in. What is he doing with our water? We need it to get home. There's no water anywhere.

Elijah stares at us and says, "Dump it out." A feverish murmur rips through the crowd.

You're pouring water onto the wood? What a waste! Why would you do that? Why throw out the little we have?

"Do it again," Elijah commands.

Watching the water splash over the stones is agony. How can we survive without water?

"Again."

Four jars poured out over twelve stones. Wood soaked and jars emptied, the water pools in the trench.

The gaunt faces are too shocked to register anger. Only despair. Before the crowd can move, Elijah prays, "'Answer me, Lord. Answer me, so these people will know you, Lord, are God, and that you are turning their hearts back again'" (1 Kings 18:37).

And then the crowd's senses are overloaded—light, sound, heat—with the strength of God.

Fire consumes everything. The altar disappears. Water, stones, dirt. Everything is incinerated. When the smoke clears, all that remains is Elijah standing in the wind.

The crowd falls to the dirt, crying out in the soul's visceral response. The Lord is God. The Lord is God.

The famine-ravaged nation of Israel needs rain. But the people standing in the crowd need God. Salvation came to Israel through choosing God.

Before God sent the rain, he sent fire.

Ring, ring. My hands were shaking, and I could barely hold the phone.

God. Is this why I'm not talking? Because I don't even know what to ask for? Because I cry out for water when I truly need fire?

I suddenly became aware of a blaze in my own heart that burned up the fear. Aching agony dissolved into beauty and freedom. An incredible lightness of being, alone with God and the wind. It was utterly profound.

And somewhat temporary. As I've previously mentioned, warrior training was like sailing a ship in a hurricane. Not much actual steering, and a lot of hanging on for dear life. But gradually—almost imperceptibly—I noticed a loosening. A relaxing of my grip. By practicing not talking, I felt something sharp within me being filed to smoothness. Mental space became available for other voices—like Scripture—to percolate in my thoughts.

And by making room for God, he freed me to love my treasure without being owned by it.

Sometimes my family vacations in beautiful rental homes. It's fabulous. I soak in the tub, lounge on the porch, and revel in the gardens. Since none of it's mine, I'm free to enjoy it fully. My own home is weighed down with responsibility. I'm the owner. I'm often too busy maintaining it to soak in the tub.

By acknowledging that my most cherished possessions—my husband, children, career—fully belong to God, I become free to love them without crippling fear of loss. I can give myself completely to those I love by serving and caring for them. But they aren't mine to own and maintain. They belong to God, the Giver of all good things.

One day I was eating grilled cheese sandwiches with my son as he was discussing green Ninjago. I studied his sweet face and the dimple that appeared when he smiled. Suddenly, he stopped talking, his big eyes sparkling. "Thanks for listening to my stories, Mom. It makes me feel good."

My breath caught in my throat. My son just thanked me for listening. Because apparently that's something I did now. His eyes were so blue and his face so open. I might've missed this moment. But I didn't.

And indescribable joy filled my soul. I couldn't imagine ever feeling this complete. This satisfied. This full of life that is truly life. I smiled back and took another bite of my sandwich. And that night, I wrote in my flower journal.

"Today this ezer-girl partied over in Eight!"

CHAPTER 7

No Time to Think When Slaying Giants

You can override a habit by willpower for a moment or two. You go to church. Read the Bible. Worship. Sing. Pray. You feel at peace with God for a moment, and then your sin habit returns. Habits eat willpower for breakfast.

—John Ortberg, *Soul Keeping*

I AM SLIGHTLY WEIRD. AND I HAVE SOME STRANGE HABITS. Don't we all?

For example, I often find myself in very serious meetings with very serious people talking about very serious things. And someone will say, "I'm not sure you heard me."

And in my head, I respond, "I can't hear you. I have a banana in my ear."

Every single time.

Those awesome few of you who know I'm quoting Ernie from *Sesame Street*—you are my tribe.

My twin brother and I were inseparable as children. It was like being born with a built-in best friend. Much of my personality was shaped by reacting to his personality. And he's a nut. Therefore, he must be to blame for my irreverent tendencies.

I react to the ingrained habits instilled during my childhood with bemused frustration and call my brother's name like Seinfeld calling out, "Newman!" It happens all the time. I work on floor A in the hospital. Every morning, when I push the button in the elevator I am compelled to say, "Aaaay," like the Fonz. Often out loud. Often next to white coated doctor-ish people.

Important doctor says, "What floor do you need?"

I respond, "Aaaay." Throat clearing. "Umm, floor A. I need floor A."

Important doctor slowly pushes button and avoids further eye contact, while I listen for the sound of my brother's laughter somewhere in the distance.

These references are very cultural. Dated. They may not make sense to you, but I know you're a strong person. If you weren't a strong person, you would have left somewhere in chapter 3. My point is that we think we're intelligent people. We believe well-formulated conscious thought informs our behavior. But most of the time, we do what we do without thinking.

Welcome to the world of habit.

Most of my job consists of straight-up behaviorism. As a therapist, I've been trained to identify a problem. Once identified, the patient's goal is to establish a new behavior to address the problem and drill the new behavior until it replaces the old one. Then a new habit is formed. Problem solved.

Yep, that's what I do. Engage in the process of fixing a problem by creating a new behavior. But I gotta tell you.

It hardly ever works.

One of my professors in graduate school—a well-respected leader in the field—gave a series of lectures on how to determine progress with valid treatment measures. She was more than qualified, having published books, authored papers, and developed an assessment battery that carried her name. In the middle of a lecture, she paused.

"In all my years of treating people, I can count the patients that I feel like I've truly helped on one hand."

Radio silence.

That's just the encouragement everyone about to join the profession of helping people wants to hear. "Hello, wannabes. I'm brilliant. I spent many years becoming brilliant. I've already forgotten more brilliant things than you currently know. And with all this wisdom, knowledge, and experience, I've helped fewer than five people. But don't worry, it's not too bad. You'll probably have a good dental plan. Good luck then. Cheerio."

But in all honesty, this shouldn't be shocking. The fact that human beings are creatures of habit, and that these habits are monstrously difficult to change, comes as a surprise to no one. Weight loss is a billion-dollar-per-year industry, people. Why? Because we are colossally uninformed about the real reasons behind why we do what we do. Getting to the heart of the issue is excruciating. And once identified, we must address the issue in new ways. This usually involves less salt, fat, and sugar. And we must do it again and again and again. Forever. It's a ton of work and fraught with danger, because at any point the old behavior is an option. To succeed, one can't be simply focused on weight loss but must be obsessed with developing within oneself the identity of someone who interacts with food with healthy indifference. The inner dialogue must change from "Should I eat this?" to "I never struggle with food because I make healthy choices without thinking."

Easy as pie. Oops, now I'm thinking about dessert.

When we walk through the doors of a weight loss program, we're willing to pay money. Willing to attend meetings, count calories, and eat broccoli. At least for a little while. But the persisting problem is we are not willing to become a different person because it's the hardest thing on earth. Habits meet needs. They soothe hurts. Fill in gaps. Stand in for missing love. There's always a reason we do what we do. We just remain predominantly ignorant of our internal motives.

Charles Duhigg wrote an epic book called *The Power of Habit.* Using research and fascinating real-life examples, Duhigg explains how our subconscious systems are responsible for the lion's share of our behaviors: "Habits are powerful, but delicate. They can emerge outside our consciousness, or can be deliberately designed. They often occur without our permission, but can be reshaped by fiddling with their parts. They shape our lives far more than we realize—they are so strong, in fact, that they cause our brains to cling to them at the exclusion of all else, including common sense."[10]

It seems logical to assume that one of the difficulties with the spiritual goal of not conforming to the patterns of the world is that we're barely aware of the patterns to begin with. And when we go about trying to change our behaviors, we're no more successful in the spiritual realm than we are in the physical. If I struggle this hard to give up ice cream before bed, what chance do I have with the red-letter sins? And what about the sins I haven't even realized I've committed? As Peg says to Cat, "I'm totally freaking out!"

Wendy Wood, provost professor of psychology and business at the University of Southern California, knows a lot about habit. Her research lab has focused on figuring out why we do what we do. Professor Wood conducted a study where participants were asked to taste and rate popcorn.[11] (As an aside, why do they never ask me to participate in popcorn-eating studies?) As predicted, the fresh popcorn was preferred over stale popcorn. In the lab environment, people in the "stale" group ate much less popcorn than those in the "fresh" group. Well, duh.

However, when the study environment changed to a movie theater, people who have a habit of eating popcorn at the movies ate just as much stale popcorn as those eating fresh. When the "stale" group was interviewed, they reported that they ate popcorn simply because they were at the movies. Taste was less important than maintaining a habit. "Our minds don't always integrate in the best way possible. Even when you know the right answer, you can't make yourself change the habitual behavior."[12]

Hmm. You only need to go to church a few Sundays in a row for confirmation of this truth.

10 Charles Duhigg, *The Power of Habit: Why We Do What We Do in Life and Business* (Toronto: Anchor Canada, 2014), 25.

11 David T. Neal, Wendy Wood, Mengju Wu, David Kurlander, "The Pull of the Past: When Do Habits Persist Despite Conflict with Motives?" SAGE Journals, Accessed January 2, 2022, https://journals.sagepub.com/doi/abs/10.1177/0146167211419863.

12 Ibid.

Wood's lab also detected that we are monstrously off target in facilitating actual life change because we aim our efforts at the wrong part of the mind. Wood studied behavior change programs like public service announcements, community workshops, physical fitness programs, and weight loss groups—places people usually go when they want to break out of a groove. Many church programs could be included here too. She discovered that these programs were successful at increasing motivation and desire but yielded poor long-term—defined as one-, three-, or five-year—results.[13]

Motivation to change resides in the *thinking* part of our minds and is responsive to information. We join, we listen, we agree. We close the program with resounding applause because we see logical reasons to do things differently. We read the handouts and set great goals. Unfortunately, once our willpower is depleted, we discover that the *habitual* brain wasn't even in the building.

Wow. All the information I read on habit definitely explained my lackluster performance as a Good Christian. Church was effective at illuminating my need to change and even mustering up my desire to change, but then I'd walk out of the service and *not* change.

My warrior training had to access that unconscious brain. When I learned to not talk and focused my effort on listening to God, I also slowed down and listened to my kids, my coworkers, my husband. There was a little bit of traction under my feet now.

Something about the spiritual disciplines tapped into the realm of my habitual self.

Dallas Willard describes spiritual disciplines as "activities in our power that enable us, by grace, to do what we cannot do by direct effort—by just 'trying.' They are required in every area of life, including the spiritual."[14]

---

13 Wendy Wood & David T. Neal, "Healthy through Habit: Interventions for Initiating & Maintaining Health Behavior Change," https://behavioralpolicy.org/wp-content/uploads/2017/05/BSP_vol1is1_Wood.pdf.

14 Dallas Willard, "How Does the Disciple Live?" https://dwillard.org/articles/how-does-the-disciple-live.

Preach it, D. W.

In other words, we engage in spiritual disciplines with our thinking brains in order to influence our habitual selves. Then God takes our effort and breaks us out of the death groove, transforming us through his life grooves into a new creation.

So clear, right? All these years, and I could've totally been writing theology books. Opportunity missed.

So far we've been talking about habits like they're bad things. Au contraire. Habits are massively powerful. Successful people pay attention to their habits. They make their subconscious brain move toward their goals, not against them. Habits are similar to power in that they're morally neutral. But habits can clearly serve holiness or sin. The work of transformation is not anti-habit. In fact, the opposite is true. Unless our habitual selves change to run on the God grooves, we're a scraggly patch of untapped potential. On this side of eternity, the flesh is weak. Even in Romans Eight. We can't make much progress toward holiness through willpower or thinking brains alone. Exhibit A: Genesis through Revelation.

Fortunately, Scripture makes it easy to see how habits can hurt or help. It's especially clear with my guy, Dave. You may know him as King David. After I left Mount Carmel, I went back to Bethlehem to hang out with Ruth's great-grandson. It was summertime, and I enjoyed how my obsessive nightly reading trickled into daytime conversations with my kids. Children are naturally interested in David because he's awesomesauce.

I decided to rebrand these compulsive reading jags into the term *3D Bible*. It sounded more intentional, like I planned to read the same thing every night until the wee hours. I consumed these stories so voraciously that the Bible truly felt three dimensional. By standing in various vantage points inside the story, I could see from different angles. In my many years of Bible reading, I'd never noticed the rawness of it all. The people actually *lived*. It was their *life*. Their children, their pain, their ability to pay the bills. They hadn't read their own story a million times. They didn't know the ending. My reading became intensely gripping, and when I started to see the characters as human, they began to feel like friends.

King David is easy to like. He's got natural charisma. His life is long, and he is the definition of an overcomer. Although his kingship is riveting, I was newly fascinated by his origin. After all, I was enrolled in school for warriors and recovering control freaks. What was it about David that made him so strong in the face of nonstop adversity?

Walking back into his childhood, it's clear Dave's habits propelled him toward God and away from the snare of the human need for status. How did that develop? Based on his birth order, Dave's a nobody. He has *seven* older brothers. This is possibly the origin of his very humble heart. You know what makes for great habit development in the domain of humility? Having seven older brothers. From day one, Dave has to do the jobs his siblings don't want to do. His brothers are older and, according to ancient Palestinian culture, far more valuable.

As the runt of the litter, Dave's opinion is irrelevant and unwanted. Because all the more substantial jobs are taken, David is sent to watch the sheep. Normally, a family wealthy enough to own sheep would hire out the shepherding. Firstborn sons—and second and third—are too important to watch sheep. But the eighth son? Well, let's save a little money. We're fresh out of other jobs on the estate, so it's the shepherd's life for Dave.

David is out in the wilderness when God sends the prophet Samuel to Jesse's house to anoint the new king. Dave isn't in the running for this appointment because the family already has an heir. And a spare. And another few spares. When Samuel calls for the lineup, no one says, "Hold up, where's David?"

Shepherding is a thankless job. Sheep are so brainless they can't even find their own food. They require 24/7 supervision thanks to their tendency to wander into holes or off cliffs. Due to this need for protection, the shepherd lives with the flock. He moves with the flock. He sleeps with the flock. And teenage Dave most certainly smells like the flock. Nothing Old Spice about it. God makes a point when he sends the heralding angels to the shepherds at the birth of his son. He sent angels to social nobodies, not the cultural elite.

I wonder how David felt about the situation. Granted, this is ancient Palestine, and there are certain things a million readings can't penetrate through my modern, Western mind. But it seems reasonable to imagine it didn't feel good to be left on the bench. Not even a consideration for the parade of sons when a spiritual celebrity stops by. But David, once called in from the wilderness, seems unperturbed. No matter where I stand in the text, Dave isn't righteously indignant. Looking closer, I see a healthy, handsome boy. Filthy dirty and smiling ear to ear. He's been busy rocking the shepherding gig. He doesn't jockey for attention or seem to enjoy the insult to the older seven brothers when he's chosen.

Blink, blink.

It seems like this kid is not only *okay* with it, he's completely unconcerned with it. He's focused on something else.

From the moment we meet him, Dave is practicing behaviors and developing habits that connect him to God. As he tromps about the Judean wilderness, he examines the trees, the grass, the flowers. What else is out here? Sheep, rocks, dirt. And oh yeah—God. Everywhere he goes, Dave sees evidence of a Creator. Lying on his back at night, he studies the firmament, and it blows him away.

David seeks God. In every lowly and mundane moment, his heart is bent on finding his Maker. This life groove goes on to dominate much of his behavior for his entire life. Perhaps this is why God calls him "a man after my own heart" (Acts 13:22). David defeats a giant, wins wars, becomes king. But his greatest accomplishment is passion for his Father.

And this is what I glean in the wilderness with Dave. While being completely ignored by humanity in the desert, he is active. He learns to take care of ungrateful beasts. And he does more than give a minimal performance. He *excels* at caring for sheep. He plays the harp to relax them as the sun goes down. He finds it relaxes him too, and he spends his evenings singing to God, telling him about every amazing experience that day. He learns a lot. He defends the hapless animals from attackers. He's still a kid, but he kills a lion and a bear with rocks and his bare hands.

Each night as Dave contemplates the lessons of the day, he realizes that Someone finds him valuable. He connects with his own Shepherd and finds satisfaction for his soul.

Dave finds his status in God. He's the eighth son, practically invisible, alone in the vast outdoors. And yet God is present, active, and personal. David experiences God's promise: "Those who seek me find me" (Proverbs 8:17). David composes songs and poems related to his experiences and his responses to God. He knows that God is real, and he wants more of him.

He doesn't waste time longing for what he doesn't have, the way I might if I were in his shoes. He found God to be more than enough. And transformation happens, not by consciously deciding to forgive God for his zero-status shepherd's life but by actively engaging in discovering God within his circumstance. By seeking God, he overcomes the soul-crushing need for worldly approval.

After he's anointed to be king, it appears that he's sent back to watch the sheep, at least for a time. As the spirit of the Lord comes upon him, David is well practiced in the habit of aligning his heart toward God. And so he goes back to the wilderness as a warrior in training. A boy who's becoming a man after God's own heart.

I wrote in my sparkle flower journal: "Warrior tip—warriors must pursue God first. No need, want, wish, or desire can come before my pursuit of God."

In the past, I'd always rushed along in David's story to the confrontation with Goliath. But now I was in warrior school, and there was a ton of education in the desert. David's behaviors—acknowledging God's sovereign work as Creator, talking to God about the day, praising God in song, keeping a written record of God's work—looked a lot like those spiritual discipline things Dallas goes on about.

Dave searches for God in his everyday circumstances. This habit helps cultivate a relentlessly positive attitude about God. Instead of saying, "I can't believe a lion attacked our flock and I almost got killed saving a stupid, stinking sheep," David says, "Wow, I had no idea what I was doing, but God gave me victory over the claws of the beast. Incredible! Glorious!"

When he gets a call from home sometime later, Jesse isn't simply checking on David's welfare. He wants Dave to run down to the battlefield to see how his brothers are doing and take them some decent food from home. Heaven only knows the quality of their military rations. "Hurry, David. Our best and brightest are out there. I can't rest until I know how they're doing."

I'm a little annoyed with Jesse. I want to insert words of comfort and admiration to Dave. Tell him everything he's accomplished to protect the flock. But Dave doesn't need the validation I require. He's been in the desert but not alone. He's been busy working but also connecting with the Source of all validation.

Dave grabs the bread and cheese and runs down to the battlefield. He wants to see what's happening there. He can hardly imagine what God's doing with real soldiers on a battlefield!

Dave's focus on the pursuit of God has shifted his paradigm so he can see life differently than I might. The food-runner incident doesn't anger or discourage him because he's too busy eagerly awaiting what God will do next. No task is too small or ridiculous in his pursuit of God.

I sat with that for some time. It seemed apparent that I couldn't seek validation by seeking God. But I could seek God and become valuable. Spiritual disciplines don't take the place of grace or provide healing or earn anyone merit. But they disrupt the patterns of this world and allow the warrior to focus on God.

I believe that our world's desperate, all-consuming craving for human validation and approval is a more deadly giant than Goliath could ever hope to be. Dave follows the way of the warrior before he even has facial hair. He allows God to use his experiences in the desert to develop his true identity, and Dave's participation made those life grooves a real thing. He is made into someone new.

Now comes a test. The warrior goes to battle. But the battlefield is filled with prestige, not just Philistines. After years of wandering the wilderness and singing to sheep, the spotlight shines on Dave. Finally, he's seen by the world.

But wars are full of unfair fighting. Dave's brothers remind him of his earthly status. "Why are you here, little brother? You're nothing and nobody. Who's watching the stupid beasts?"

Dave's brothers are such jerks. I want to smack them in the teeth.

Then King Saul of Israel hears about Dave down at camp.

Saul's a conflicted guy. He knows this seems like a suicide mission, but he also knows what God's capable of doing. Saul doesn't have the courage to fight Goliath, but maybe this kid does. This could work. At the very least, maybe the death of this young innocent will fire up the courage of the troops. If he chooses to send Dave to his doom, Saul must look like he was trying to protect the boy. More than anything else, Saul is destroyed by his need for approval.

Saul offers David his own armor—his royal prestige. If you're going to die fighting a giant, at least look fabulous doing it. What an excruciating moment. Dave's being handed everything most people want. Attention, renown, revenge. He could've said, "Do you see me, Eliab? Abinadab? Shimeah? Go watch Dad's sheep, you cowards. This king sees me. He put his armor on me. That's right, boys. I'm at the front of the chow line. How do you like me now?"

He could've acted like that. But he didn't.

In this adrenaline-fueled moment, if Dave had to consciously think, "What is the right thing to do?" or "How can I be a pleasing and holy sacrifice right now?" there's *no way* he would've succeeded. Maybe with a few days to reflect, pray, or study, Dave could muster up some holiness. But this is happening in real time. He simply reacts.

Dave responds the way his habitual self was developed in the desert. Thanks to all that training, a new and improved David has been made by God for this moment. He's shocked that anyone would be allowed to defy the name of God in this way and live to tell the tale. If no one else would fight the giant, David will. He's sure of one thing: If God can kill ravaging predators in defense of sheep, Dave can logically conclude that he'll kill giants in defense of his holiness.

Dave tries moving around inside Saul's armor. No dice. He removes it. "Take this stuff off. It's not who I am."

He knows his identity. That's what freedom of the soul looks like. And that's the moment Dave wins.

The battle is won before stepping onto the field. Where do I get that strength? I want it.

My sparkle flower journal started to fill up fast. Feeling joyful about these new discoveries found in what I thought was a worn story, I babbled on to my kids. I described how David really won. How all the hard work—the excruciating, giant-killing work—had been done with God before even going to battle.

My excitement got them excited because attitude is contagious. And they found tolerance for a mother who was fond of running around inside Bible stories, talking about King David as if he were sitting on the sofa. I walked along the battlefields while holding their little hands. We wondered aloud about giants. On lovely summer evenings, we waded in the creek by our house and collected giant-killing stones, stockpiling them in the backyard. They were too young to see the giants standing all around us.

I don't mean to over spiritualize things. We were mostly just busy. Eating, doing laundry, saving money at Walmart. A great percentage of life is monotony.

One afternoon, I asked my daughter to hang up her coat—something I'd asked her to do three times a day since she was old enough to stand. I had explained 7,654 times how dropping one's coat on the floor wasn't acceptable.

But instead of my usual lecture, I sank to the floor next to her little self. Her blond hair was a wild mess. The syrup from last night's pancake dinner had created angry tangles that framed her face in uneven lumps. I think she'd slept in her clothes. There was no taming this one. Her eyes—fierce and free—stared at me defiantly. I took a deep breath and tried to give the not-talking thing some space. "Babe."

I resisted the urge to smooth her hair. "Why do you think it might be important to hang up your coat?"

She hesitated. She hadn't expected a question. The deviation from our well-worn script threw her off. She sighed. "I don't know."

I sighed too. How could she possibly not know? I had corrected her a million times.

I looked into her downcast face. Motherhood is insanely hard, but then so is childhood.

She wiggled around while sitting next to me, like a wild thing in a box. Then she spoke, eyes fixed on the wall. "Maybe coats are like bread and cheese."

What? I tried to catch up. Were we talking about lunch? I bit my tongue and let the silence linger.

"Like David." She examined her dirty fingernails. "David took the bread and cheese to his brothers because he learned to obey God." She reached her hand haphazardly toward her pink coat, adding, "The bread and cheese wasn't the important part."

"Right," I said, trying hard to not ruin the moment with a teary flood of parenting bliss. "Right."

That night I scribbled away in my sparkle flower journal.

"Warrior tip: the bread and cheese were never the important part. Habits, correctly formed, move the body without thought in reckless, wonderful pursuit of God. Also note, there is currently a small pink jacket hanging by the door."

CHAPTER 8

God or Not God

Trust is accepting what God sends into your life whether you understand it or not. Putting our faith in Christ is not about trying harder; it means transferring our trust away from ourselves and resting in him.

—Timothy Keller, *Shaped by the Gospel: Doing Balanced, Gospel-Centered Ministry in Your City*

WARRIOR TRAINING WAS HARD WORK. IT WAS TOUGH TO remember everything in real time, mostly because the rest of the world wasn't cooperating. At the end of the day, there was much more Romans Seven to write about in my journal than Eight.

And now we know why monks retreat to secluded places. People can be jerks. And unfortunately, sometimes when I'm around other jerks, I become a jerk. Osmosis happens.

In case you weren't listening in seventh grade, osmosis explains a lot. We are all semipermeable barriers. Our opinions, behavior, and values are vastly influenced by our immediate environment. When I'm in the world, I soak it up like a dry sponge in a puddle. The dryness of the sponge actually attracts water. That is how I'm able to spend all morning in the Beatitudes and then tell off the lunch lady when she mischarges me for mashed potatoes. And not even notice the disconnect. I fancy that the core of who I am is cemented in my soul like a bank vault, when in actuality the boundaries of my psyche are more like velvet rope barriers in the lobby.

Yep. The monks are on to something. If the end goal is sin-free living, better move to the wasteland. Avoid people at all costs. It's vastly easier to love thy neighbor as thyself if the closest neighbor is 839 miles away. Flee temptation. Get rid of everything—television, Wi-Fi, double caramel macchiatos—because Romans Seven is alive and well.

I am a dry sponge that craves acknowledgment. Let's flesh that out, shall we? I am a people lover. No, that's not quite right. I want to be loved by people. Yes, that's it. From birth I have wanted to be liked, respected, and admired. One of the initial byproducts of warrior training was the painful and clarifying picture of my rejection of God's authority in pursuit of—what exactly? Popularity? Am I really that shallow?

Yes. Yes, I am.

And for this, I partially blame my brothers.

My earliest memories involve the pursuit of acclaim. I was born at the end of a long line of talented brothers. They won everything. They were born to win. A simple game of Monopoly—wait, there's no such thing as a simple game of Monopoly—would result in hours-long, agonizing negotiations to win Park Place away from their much younger sister. In sports, they lettered in everything. And in the hallowed halls of Ralston High School, my brothers were living legends. Everywhere I went, people would learn my last name and immediately ask, "Oh, do you know Bud?" or "Aren't you Randy's little sister?"

From day one, I was a fierce competitor. My habitual self had a drive for glory before I could even spell the word. It was kind of an awesome childhood. I ran around believing I was a superhero. I wasn't afraid to try anything, and most of the time I'd succeed.

My dad breathed Norman Vincent Peale and the power of positive thinking. If God is for you, who can be against you? Know who you are and go conquer.

Confidence is all we really need, and I had plenty of it.

Then one summer I headed off to camp with a body like Skipper but came home in the shape of Barbie. I didn't slowly blossom,

I exploded. And then I entered junior high—the biggest playing field of my life—and it was fraught with peril because suddenly my confidence was gone. And an enemy called self-doubt appeared.

You could write a hundred books about the battleground that is junior high. Everything familiar was gone, and I was a stranger in a strange land. Even my own body became totally foreign.

At the time, I didn't know why my confidence disappeared. But somewhere on the rocky road of puberty, the game changed. It was no longer about winning to win. It was about winning so that *others* knew I was a winner. This is the primary takeaway from junior high. It's crucial to be seen. If you can't make people like you, make them fear you. If you can't be loved, be hated. Anything is better than anonymity. Ask any seventh grader—the lessons continue today.

This subconscious groove goes deep. Our entire society revolves around the fear of being obscure.

It turns out that Maslow was right.

Abraham Maslow is the psychologist famous for organizing the order of human needs into a nifty triangle.[15] He ordered them into levels—just like Mario Brothers. The needs that form the first level at the base of the triangle are food, water, and shelter. Above that is safety, or assurance that you won't be robbed of your basic needs. Then we move up the triangle to the need for loving relationships. Sharing our lives with others is a human requirement, prevalent across all cultures. Next, Maslow argues we have the need to be esteemed, valued, and respected. Finally, the tip of the triangle is self-actualization. This essentially means reaching our full potential, or as Maslow calls it, becoming fully human.

Naturally, if a person is hungry, they're less concerned about the *in crowd* because they're focused on getting food in the belly. However, if the food need is continually met, they can concentrate on being safe, with a place to sleep and do laundry, before moving up again.

15 W. Huitt, "Maslow's Hierarchy of Needs," https://www.coursehero.com/file/123618105/Educational-Psychology-Interactive-Maslows-hierarchy-of-needspdf/.

But before they can win the game, they must achieve the esteem level. Wikipedia—fount of wisdom for lazy students everywhere—tells us Maslow's Esteem Level includes the quest for self-respect and respect from others. And in our culture, we've associated esteem with beauty, wealth, strength, power, etc.

If you like, you can sign up for a psychology course. Sit through hours of lectures, take notes, use highlighters. Cram for exams that require an obscene amount of caffeine to remain focused. And then finally, fling yourself on the mercy of extra credit by volunteering to be a research subject for grad students. This is how I got a front-row seat into the human quest for self worth based on acknowledgment.

Or you can just grab a Diet Coke and read a few issues of *People* magazine.

Either way, the principle will become strikingly clear. The human need for acknowledgment runs the Western world. It's not enough to win. Others must know that you're the winner, or it doesn't count. Seriously, I've just saved you from hours of lectures. You're welcome.

The need to be seen is a deep groove in our hearts, and it's almost impossible to dislodge. I rest my case on Field Day. In the eighties, self-esteem was a hot topic. Suddenly, everyone became very concerned about self-esteem, especially the self-esteem of children. Thanks to Field Day, I vividly remember the switch to focusing on self-worth. It was abrupt, to say the least.

If you never had the pleasure of participating in Field Day BSE—Before Self-Esteem—allow me to explain. Field Day was awesome. We got to go to the high school stadium, where the big kids did real sports. And more importantly, it took up an entire day of school. No math, no language arts, no social studies. It was like Christmas in June. Field Day consisted of about a dozen different track and field events. We competed against our classmates, and the student who got first place received a blue ribbon. Second place earned a red ribbon. Third place, white. Then yellow, green, and pink. I still remember all the colors—and the passionate chase for blue.

Then self-esteem happened. On a brilliant blue Nebraskan morning, the fifth grade got on the bus and rumbled out to the high school stadium. We competed in the events—softball throw, long jump, hundred-yard dash—and then settled onto the field to enjoy a Popsicle while the awards were distributed. I hadn't even finished my cherry bomb before the teachers finished threading through our ranks, handing each of us a blue ribbon with crisp gold lettering that read *Participant.*

Confusion reigned. "But who won?" we demanded.

And Mrs. Hays announced with the air of a wizened sage, "You're all winners today."

We were stunned. Wait, what?

As we filed off the bus after Field Day was over, I spied multiple blue ribbons lying discarded between the vinyl seats.

Sigh.

Just to be clear, implying that all children are winners and that Field Day was about sportsmanship and the value of each person was totally honorable. It's a reflection of Scripture and found all over Romans Eight. The problem was that Mockingbird Elementary was not living in the land of Eight. We lived and breathed and grew up in Seven, and Field Day reinforced this paradigm. You can switch the color of the ribbon. You can call everyone a winner. But without a corresponding paradigm shift, we all were left feeling a bit cheated.

Whether we understood the impact of this culture shift is debatable. It's hard for the fish to judge the quality of the water. But *everyone is a winner* is a sentiment that will never survive outside the walls of primary school because from the perspective of the life traveler, it's simply not true. The tallest, the prettiest, the smartest, the wealthiest, the most athletic—these are the winners. Children aren't easily fooled. The abandoned ribbons on the bus proved it.

One of my biggest hurdles was that I didn't understand my life's focus couldn't be on worldly success. My allegiance to Jesus would put me at odds with the world from the very start. If I desired a ribbon from the world, no amount of ribbons from God would fill the void.

The self-esteem confusion persisted into the 1990s. As writer and reviewer Rebecca Nappi observes, the entire decade was dedicated to self-help and learning to love and appreciate your inner person. Apparently, you didn't need the approval of the world if you learned to love yourself. M. Scott Peck, Wayne Dyer, and Susan Powter were all *New York Times* best-selling authors[16] who sold millions of books informing us exactly how we could overcome our inner snags and press onward to victory. The whole country believed that with hard work and self-control, we could both conquer the world and save it.

I remember standing in my homecoming dress when my mother said, "Beauty comes from the inside out. Just wait and see."

I waited. And waited. But no one noticed my inner beauty at homecoming. Maybe I was shy or didn't believe in myself enough. It was a different night for my classmate, Megan Dean. She went home with a crown on her head. And the lesson was clear—you can call yourself a princess all you want, but until someone actually puts a crown on your head, you're dreaming.

Hindsight is harsh to even the very best self-esteem soothsayers. Susan Powter, whose battle cry was "Stop the Insanity," went bankrupt. Dr. M. Scott Peck wrote on the virtues of a disciplined life and delayed gratification before he eventually confessed to cheating on his wife during their entire marriage. And Wayne Dyer, after publishing his book telling others how to "change your thoughts, change your life," experienced three failed marriages. Perhaps the insanity can't be stopped, the gratification can only be delayed for so long, and finding the right thoughts to change is harder than it looks.

This is only an observation about these writers, not a judgment. If people absolutely dedicated to the journey of self-improvement can struggle so mightily, what hope is there for the rest of us?

With any genuine self-reflection, even the dimmest bulb can see that living for oneself is not the best way. Self-gratification is empty,

16 Rebecca Nappi, "Pondering the Self-Help Books Written during the 1990s," *The Spokesman-Review*, December 30, 2010, https://www.spokesman.com/stories/2011/jan/02/powerless-to-change/.

like chasing the wind. Thank you, King Solomon. But when push comes to shove, we tend to push and shove to get our needs met. And then once the burger is in the belly, we push and shove to make ourselves valuable and seen. Anything besides obscurity.

It's what we do. It's what we were born into.

The world doesn't play by God's rules. Our culture teaches us, preaches to us, and demands that we are not neutral on this point: God's way is stupid.

Every day, from cradle to grave, we live with a law of humanity that is contrary to God's teaching.

Every person cannot be a winner. Only the winner is the winner.

Participant ribbons are for losers.

God seems unreasonable when he states that we cannot be both his friend and a friend of the world. Isn't that the lie the snake sold to Eve? It's unfair for God to expect we wouldn't want to better ourselves and our situation.

Here's where it gets tricky. It's easy to feel like God is talking to those outside the fold. Christians approach love of the world with an us-versus-them mentality. Clearly, we are on God's side. And the pagans, Democrats, and environmentalists are over there on the other side. They see God as foolish. But we're his children, and we're on Team God. It's all about our definition of self. I define myself as a good person because I am a Christian.

We may not say this out loud, but our behavior indicates our belief is that good people do good things for good reasons. If I do something good for a good reason, then the Bible says God will bless me. In this way, I'm more than a conqueror because God's on my side. This is the essence of "name it and claim it" religion.

The problem is that I can't actually find that verse in my Bible. Instead, I find a whole bunch of disturbing Scriptures that define being governed by the Spirit as dying to self. It doesn't matter what I do, even if it's awesome. Even if I cure cancer or bring fresh water to thousands of African children or choose to be nice to my coworker who shamelessly takes credit for my work.

If Jesus wasn't the reason I did it, then it doesn't count.

And in this brutally honest moment, I admit it. Jesus is never the reason. Not the real reason. Not really. I do what I do so I'll be acknowledged. On my very best Romans Seven Self day, I do what I do so that God will see me do it. Look, God. See what I did there? I earned a gold star today.

When God says it's impossible to be friends with the world, he's not talking to the pagans. He's talking to his children.

Because it's not us versus them. It's us versus *us*. Flesh versus spirit. Seven versus Eight. Death versus life. And that's why moving to the wasteland only works temporarily.

Because there's no zip code where you don't exist when you are there.

Let's sit with that for a minute. I may need more coffee.

So we operate within the grooves of our culture. Externally, we do good things so people will see it and appreciate it and maybe click "like." Internally, we do good things so God will see it and maybe give us a thumbs-up. And because we're blind to our real nature, we bring all the rules of the world inside the church, and it gets all kinds of dysfunctional as we run around hoping people will notice our holiness. Naturally, we hide our brokenness. *That* stuff shouldn't just be splashed all over the place. Better save that for the unspoken prayer requests.

Without the requirement of transformation as evidence of right with God, the church grows weak, inept, and dangerous. At least we understand the game we play in the junior high lunchroom, but here in church, we profess one thing and do another. Like a hospital that kills the wounded.

Our Christian life is supposed to be a race. A battle. It requires effort. But in today's church, there's little spiritual sweat. It's like Field Day all over again, minus the refreshing frozen treat. It's no real mystery why the participant ribbon the church offers us is not very motivating. Who's the real winner? Us? God? The lost? I don't know.

Exactly.

The only way to win spiritually is to figure out who's sovereign in our lives. If it's God, then we must follow him. Live and breathe and bleed like he did. If it's ourselves, then why do the church thing? Doing that without pursuing God is equivalent to putrescence. It's in the Bible. Look it up.

So back to little Hollylu, the girl who once had confidence in herself. Then she was put through the crucible of junior high, where she wondered, "If personal value comes from outside myself, the world must value me for my behavior to count as a win. I love Jesus. But his ways don't really mesh with my culture. I'm confused. I want a win/win. To love God *and* love the mall."

Because little Hollylu didn't know that Christianity was never synonymous with comfortable. She knew that she loved God, but she also craved the affection of her culture more than anything found in church. So she tried to blend the two. She pulled a lot of Christian behaviors into her desire to be liked by the world. And over time, this eventually made her—yep—a Good Christian.

Fast forward. Now I'm trying to break out of this Good Christian groove. I discover I was made to be a warrior, but deep down inside a warrior is the need to *win*, so what am I supposed to do with that? How can I win at the game of mortification? Pretty sure that's an oxymoron. And if my role as a sacrifice is to give myself up, where does my esteem come from? According to the Gospel of Maslow, I need to feel valued before I can reach my full potential.

Sigh. Of course, we know the Sunday school answer. Our value comes from God. He found us so valuable that he didn't even spare his beloved son to save us.

God's love for us gives us value. Jesus's work on the cross creates Romans Eight living. But until we stop craving the blue ribbons of the world, we will never fully appreciate the sacrificial, overwhelming, world-dominating love of God.

It seemed clear from the summaries in my journal, which I now referred to as the Sparkle Flower Journal of Awesomeness, that unplugging from the world's blue-ribbon system was the next step in warrior training. My thoughts filled with visions of weird fashion and minimalist makeup.

Ring, ring. Hello, God. I see we have come to an understanding that I need to detach more from the world. But let the record reflect that I'm not wearing my hair in a bun. Because that gives me a headache, and it's not very slimming for my body type.

Long pause.

You know. In case you were going to ask me to do that. Just being up front. Amen.

Long. Journey. Ahead.

There is simply no way to write this and make myself sound in any way noble. In fact, three words that best describe my growth in this area are *kicking and screaming*. It was a slow, lonely road. I always wanted to read a book written by a person who recognized her incredible level of shallowness—who lived in the land of plenty but always wanted plenty more. I wanted to read how this girl eventually came to terms with her gross vanity and allowed God to make her deep waters. And I wanted the deepness to redeem the shallowness, not eliminate it. Because it's one thing to buy a new house, but it's quite another to make an ugly house beautiful.

Yeah, not a big market for that story. Perhaps because when shallow-gone-deep girl gets to the place where God's giving the blue ribbons, her desire to be seen by the world—like writing a book that people will talk about—has disappeared. Or maybe I've read these stories, and I couldn't see because I wore my old glasses. A good example was *Passion and Purity: Learning to Bring Your Love Life under Christ's Control* by Elisabeth Elliot. Mrs. Laeger selected it as a devotional for my youth group. Bless her.

Elisabeth Elliot talked about waiting on God to meet her needs. She waited on God for a husband, and God eventually provided an amazing one in Jim Elliot. But when her husband was bringing God's Word to the lost people in a foreign nation, he was speared to death by natives. And Elisabeth was left alone with their ten-month-old baby and an opportunity to wait on God some more. I flung the book at my bedroom wall and actually ran screaming from the room. I couldn't see the freedom Elisabeth was talking about. I couldn't see a life filled with blue ribbons from God—a life filled with joy, peace, and contentment. All I could see was an impossible faith that recklessly believed in God despite devastating circumstances.

Seven can never understand Eight. Just give it up. God will never, *ever* make sense to our human ways of thinking. *Gah!*

God had to lead one tiny step at a time—in the fog, over rocky terrain—with a hugely inept and largely unwilling participant.

Turns out that's his preferred method.

In that time of stumbling about in the murkiness of understanding that God was in control and I would never be, I often headed over to Jericho. Joshua's surge into the Promised Land inspired me. It comforted and reassured. It was way more fun to watch God's big moment than to contemplate the wandering desert life. Or to see the gradual fadeout in Second Kings. I wanted to be like Josh. Who wouldn't want to be like him? This guy hardly puts a foot wrong in his entire journey with God.

But Josh's story intersected with the story of an antihero of sorts, and it caught my attention in a new way. So I started hanging out in the cathouse. You heard me. The brothel, the house of ill repute, Naughtyville.

I had watched Jericho fall many times. But I hadn't walked around inside the city before the walls fell. God's enemy was my enemy. Why would I hang out there? But I had watched the parade around the city enough. One day, I just snuck in with the spies instead of waiting in the camp.

Inside Jericho's gates, an oppressive fear hovers over the city. From the top of the impressively fortified walls, I can see the Israelites camping just across the Jordan. All 2.5 million of them. The smoke from their fires blows up the hill and stalls over the city. My breathing becomes labored.

Fear and chaos reign inside the city. Nerves fray. Storm troopers clomp down alleyways looking for intruders. Society is unraveling.

With impending doom a mere stone's throw away, people are busy trying to take care of number one.

The Israeli spies duck into Rahab's House of Comforts like strangers plowing through the swinging doors of an Old West saloon. Everyone inside has their own worries. No one makes eye contact.

Rahab is determined to do whatever it takes to survive. She considers the facts. The God of Israel is said to be all powerful. The citizens of Jericho, even those with money and clout, are melting in fear of this God. And Rahab has heard the rumors of the Red Sea parting and escapees from Egypt walking through on dry land. For unknown reasons, the Israelites had been hiding somewhere in the desert for the past four decades. And now, after wiping the map with the Amorites, they pitched their tents outside of Rahab's hometown.

She spots the spies from across the bar. These fresh faces stick out like sore thumbs. She doesn't care about them, but is there a way to profit here? If she turns the spies over to the king, there's sure to be a payday. She knows the royal thugs will barge through the door momentarily. Working against the speed of gossip, Rahab plays the game. She quickly hides the newcomers under the flax drying on the roof.

When the Jericho storm troopers stomp into the saloon, Rahab's ready. Shirt unbuttoned and beer on tap, she lies like a rug. "Oh, rats. You big, handsome guys just missed 'em. Hurry, you might catch 'em if you get out of the city gates before they're locked."

When the obtuse Jericho task force is locked outside the city at dusk, Rahab confronts the young spies hiding on the roof. She plays her hand. "Listen up, boys. Nothing is more powerful than your God, so tell him to cut me in. A life for a life. When you roll over Jericho, let my family and me live. Swear by your God that you'll do this."

And they do swear. If she leaves a red rope hanging from the window, and her family stays inside the home, they'll ask God to spare her.

And then they leave.

The plan is in place. Now she and her family wait. Three weeks later the Israelites cross the Jordan, and Jericho freaks out. They prepare for a lengthy siege. Unlike most cities, Jericho has a freshwater spring inside the walls. The citizens fill the cisterns full of grain. Locking up the gates, they hunker down. Ready to wait years if needed.

And Rahab sits inside her house, a red rope dangling from her window. She isn't visited by an angel. She knows nothing of Joshua's plan. She only knows of God, and she's bet everything on him.

On the first day, there's murmuring. Has the siege begun? No. The Israelites only marched around the city blowing horns and then returned to their camp. How strange.

Rahab's mother asks, "Why are we here, Rahab? Is the red rope a good idea, honey? Are you sure about this?"

Day two, same deal. Circle, toot the horn, then back to camp. What is this?

If Rahab is tempted to leave the house, check up on the plan, or take some other action—rather than this passive path to salvation—it isn't recorded. Rahab's cards have been called, and everyone stares at her stony face.

The door stays locked.

Her family grows impatient. The game of cat and mouse is soundly detested by mice everywhere. Rahab's brother asks in disgust, "Why don't they just get it over with?"

The days tick by with agonizing slowness. The sound of marching is terrifying in the eerie silence that blankets Jericho. The ram's horn is the most chilling sound any resident has ever heard.

I know what happens on the seventh day, but the people in this small apartment do not. They're pale with fear. Paralyzed by the vigil. No one eats. No one sleeps.

Finally, I crack. I crouch next to Rahab and ask, "How can you stand this? This waiting and uncertainty. This makes no sense at all."

And she looks up at me with the face of a Wall Street banker. "The deal was to wait inside the house. I made the deal. Now I wait."

This isn't what I thought confidence in God would look like. I figured there would be a ray of light falling on her face or a look of rapture in her eyes. But this seems like stubbornness. Maybe Rahab should be praying. Or knitting. She looks like an obstinate child who is done walking and flatly refuses to move. It's not heroic; it's fatalistic.

Here in this dark apartment, the oppressive silence interrupted only by the wail of the shofar, I see that Rahab has embraced Christ following in its purest form. Rahab knows what the Good Christian doesn't understand. God doesn't need our help.

Rahab believes that God is the all-powerful Creator of the universe. She contributes nothing. But her confidence is in this: "If God is who I think he is, then this is the only way forward." And it saves her.

Rahab understands the long game. She sees people out in the desert who serve a God who defies all understanding, while inside the city gates the status quo melts with fear. Rahab doesn't know right from wrong. She only knows God from *not* God. And she chooses God. And all these things will be added unto her.

In Rahab—a stubborn girl with little worldly value—I see Jesus talking about the kingdom of God. The first will be last, and the last will be first. The wealthy will be poor, and the poor will be wealthy. When Jesus came, he inverted everything. To gain your life, you must lose it. To experience freedom, you must embrace slavery. The blue ribbons of the world—wealth, fame, prestige, beauty—are meaningless. The blue ribbons of God—joy, peace, rest, contentment—are priceless.

Rahab gets it. If this God is all powerful, then she'll strike her deal with him. Her résumé doesn't matter. Her past experience doesn't matter. She won't attempt to assist God in her salvation. She will wait, and he will deliver her.

Rahab is scandalously listed in the genealogy of Jesus. And in Hebrews chapter 11—the Hall of Faith—Rahab is listed by name, while Joshua is only alluded to in the mention of Jericho. Interesting.

It used to bother me that Rahab couldn't shake her reputation. Rahab, the soiled one. As a kid I thought "Theharlot" was her last name, but now I get it. The kingdom is here. The status quo is shattered, the pecking order is inverted, and the bad girl is *in*. Why? Same reason anyone is in. She placed her confidence in the right place.

So what about warrior training? If the apostle Paul wants me to work hard—but work hard in the *right way*—how am I supposed to do that? As a Good Christian, I was certainly working hard but not transforming much. But if God does the transforming, could he please speed up the glacially slow process?

My time with Rahab was valuable. It seemed as if the moral of the story wasn't so much about right or wrong. That's murky water because lots of right behavior with wrong motives equals Nicodemus in the night. While Rahab didn't appear to know much of right or wrong, she certainly figured out God from *not* God.

I resolved to begin approaching life this way as well—God or *not* God?

It was possible to have drinks in a bar with coworkers and find a lot of God. It was also possible to attend a prayer meeting and experience mostly *not* God.

If I was going to unplug from the world's blue-ribbon system, I had to not only seek more of God, but I also had to ruthlessly identify and reject *not* God. This is where the spiritual disciplines would assist in warrior training. Dallas Willard, Richard Foster, and other authors have sorted the disciplines into two categories. One is pursuit—prayer, Bible reading, fellowship, etc.—and the second is retreat—fasting, silence, solitude, etc.

Identifying God would be found in the disciplines of pursuit. Finding and rejecting *not* God would be found through the disciplines of retreat.

All my efforts to move forward were thwarted by the million invisible strings tying me to the blue-ribbon world grooves in my soul. But now I had a string detector. Switching to God or *not* God thinking illuminated behavior in ways never seen before.

And God slowly and patiently led me forward in the fog.

I discovered in warrior training that it wasn't so much about knowing the destination as it was about trusting the Leader.

We are trusting the Leader wherever he may go.

CHAPTER 9

The Transmogrified Life

Why is it that some Christians, although they hear many sermons, make but slow advances in the divine life? Because they neglect their closets, and do not thoughtfully meditate on God's Word. They love the wheat, but they do not grind it.

—Charles Spurgeon, *Morning and Evening*

RAHAB ROCKED MY WORLD. THE REDEFINITION OF SURRENDER. The *all-in* behavior that refused to budge. The cutting away of all that is *not* God.

And this is the conundrum of the ages. How to be *in* the world but not *of* it. What does that mean, really? Put down your concordance. I know the Sunday school answer. We're supposed to live inside Romans Eight while Romans Seven rails day and night against the kingdom of God. The key to doing this is to become so filled with positive pressure—so much of Jesus—that the negative draw ceases to exist. A saturated sponge dropped into a puddle can't take in any more water.

Yes. That's the answer. But what does that look like? How does the sponge get so full that it can only drain out, rather than take in? That's a Bible study I would take. I don't know how to live in a world filled with jerky, crappy people—understanding I'm just as jerky and crappy—but be so full of God's grace that when someone cuts in the coffee line, I don't feel a negative thought. Not even one.

When I read my Bible with any sort of integrity, I realize this is the goal. Not the right behavior but the right *mind*. A mind that flows only one way.

My warrior training reached a plateau at this point. I could see the destination. But every step landed me in the same place. Treading water is frustrating. When it comes to the development of a God-grooved mind, all my years of religious training were colossally unhelpful.

And I think it's because we treat our religious behaviors like a Duplicator when what we really need is a Transmogrifier.

Allow me to explain. Almost everything we need to know about the foibles and frailty of mankind can be gleaned from a serious study of Calvin and Hobbes. Not the philosophers from the Middle Ages, but the comic strip about a boy and his stuffed tiger.

Calvin and Hobbes was published from the mid-1980s to the mid-1990s. It featured a seven-year-old boy as the antihero and his stuffed tiger as the affable commentator on Calvin's true source of motivation. The creator, Bill Watterson, is some sort of anthropological genius.

Calvin unabashedly lives in Romans Seven. He serves himself. Watterson named his little despot after John Calvin, the theologian whose teaching on the innate sin nature reinforced the Augustine concept that humans are born with a desire to sin. We are literally bent toward evil. Calvin's best friend, Hobbes, is a stuffed tiger who is also purposefully named. Thomas Hobbes was a seventeenth-century English philosopher best known for his views on how humans might live in harmony with other humans and avoid the many downfalls caused by humanity in general.

These two—the boy and his stuffed tiger—illuminate our fight to be our own god. In addition, they shed light on why churches everywhere have a hard time running successful small-group ministries. In our selfish humanity, the neediness of others is annoying.

I could talk for days about the awesomeness of this comic strip, but let's focus—because focus is good—on the Duplicator and the Transmogrifier.

The Duplicator is a magical cardboard-box invention that creates a clone of whatever is put inside it. Calvin, like many great inventors, is motivated by laziness. He believes there must be a better way to get chores done than to slog through the process every single day, so he creates the Duplicator. Finally, a way to reap reward without the work. He invents a machine that makes a duplicate of himself. Calvin simply steps inside, Hobbes pushes a button, and voilà! Another Calvin is created. Clone Calvin is then assigned all the unwanted jobs that Original Calvin would like to avoid. Make the bed. Rake the leaves. Math homework. In theory, it was a perfect plan.

But Clone Calvin is, well, a clone. He doesn't want to work any more than Original Calvin does. Unexpectedly, Clone Calvin goes into the Duplicator and creates a clone of Clone Calvin. And now we're off to the races. Please note that Original Calvin never intended a clone to eat candy or go to the park. He wants the duplicate to do the hard work while *he* takes it easy. The Clone Calvins run amok, leaving Original Calvin—with Hobbes's help—to restore order by eliminating all the duplicates. Eventually, the boy and his tiger corral all the Clone Calvins back into the box, which is newly labeled "Transmogrifier."

The Transmogrifier is completely different from the Duplicator. In the Transmogrifier, what goes into it is different from what comes out. The original transforms into something entirely new. Calvin transmogrifies his cloned selves into earthworms and then releases them into the backyard.

What's my point here?

If church is the cardboard box, then many of us visit the Duplicator every week.

We go. We sit and listen. We might even take notes, and then we leave. At the very best, we have gained a duplicate version of a truth first given to the speaker. Our original self remains unaltered. Our original self wants to coast along on the work of others.

It's not just the church building. It's also Bible study, Christian radio, and Christian culture in general. It's much easier to sit in the Duplicator. I'd like to benefit from someone else's work with God. Great sermon, great song, great devotional. I can sit through these things and come out the other side unchanged.

The Transmogrifier doesn't duplicate; it makes something new. The only way to know the Transmogrifier is working is to *change*.

There's no transmogrifying by proxy. I have to get into the box myself, do the hard work with God, and learn firsthand.

And this is where my efforts in warrior training stalled. It was much easier to lean on the work of others. I didn't realize I was using them as a substitute. Going to church, serving the needy, reading dusty copies of Jonathan Edwards. I could fill my schedule with godly things like nobody's business.

But then I'd have a really bad day or a health scare or witness someone I loved in crisis. Or sometimes I would inexplicably behave in ways that filled me with shame. I'd run toward sin like a dog returning to its vomit. On those days, it was impossible to stand firm. Fear gripped my soul and shook my resolve. Like a person climbing out from under the debris following a hurricane, I stood blinking in the sun, surveying the damage.

The lack of progress was discouraging. It turns out that even while attending Warrior Training Night School—with its surrendering and 3D Bible reading—I wasn't really very different from the last time the wind blew the house down.

I wanted a new me. I desired the kingdom of God to spread across my heart. It just didn't seem to be progressing very quickly, despite serious effort on my part.

I must've missed something.

Well, I probably missed lots of things. Working on my weaknesses was like shooting fish in a barrel. But as I worked through the disciplines of retreat, I noticed that two particular practices were more loathsome than the rest. So much so that I'd find elaborate reasons to skip my assignments or shorten them or do something else and call it good.

I detest silence and solitude. For heaven's sake, I wasn't even alone in the womb. When I'm by myself at home, I always turn at least one television on and the radio and maybe a podcast too. So when I try to sit quietly, alone and supposedly focused on listening to God, all I hear is static. Static, buzzing, and a few bizarre and meaningless thoughts. Silence is a very chaotic experience for me. I'm also hardwired for constant movement and stimulation. Yet both of these spiritual discipline twins—silence and solitude—involve sitting quietly before God with zero agenda.

I'll give my time, my energy, maybe even my money. I'll do the other disciplines twice—just please don't ask me to sit in silence or solitude.

Until now, my warrior training had involved discovering God's agenda. Making God's agenda my agenda. But here in these challenging disciplines of retreat, I was asked to lay down my clipboard and spend time with God.

Sounds so simple. The problem was that this required spending time with myself. My brain, my heart, and my motives. God didn't speak loudly or in any way that captured my attention. All I experienced was my bizarre self running around in my thoughts like an unrestrained bull in a china shop. It's no wonder I avoided silence. Who wants to invite chaos into conscious thought?

But I was determined to push through. I stubbornly set a time goal and forced myself to sit through it. Five minutes of silence was exhausting. No judging, Judgy McJudgerson. I'd bail out around three minutes and read Scripture for the remaining time. If God wasn't going to fill the excruciating silence, at least I could listen to him through his Word.

One day, after not even cracking three minutes, I sighed in disgust. I didn't know why I persisted in this. Wasn't it enough to read the Bible? Why did I need to sit silently before my Creator? Maybe I could just write *good effort* on the silence and solitude report card.

That evening, I wandered back to Elijah at Mount Carmel. No matter how many times I read it, I was awestruck. But that night, we kept going. Elijah trash talks Ahab. Filled with the power of God, he races against the king's chariots and beats them back to town. On *foot.*

And then everything shifts. Jezebel says she's going to kill him. She has a reputation for killing people, so this shouldn't come as a surprise to anyone. But Elijah deflates. Slowly, he fills with fear, and then he quits. Really? Talk to me, Elijah. What's going on? But Elijah doesn't answer me. He closes up shop and heads into the desert.

Elijah has post-fire-on-mountaintop depression. How anticlimactic. Why is crisis coming after the victory? Elijah, listen to your own sermon tapes. Don't you remember what God just did?

We sat by the broom bush. It was hard to recognize this man as the one who stood powerfully in the wind a few passages ago—the one who prayed for rain seven times when there wasn't a cloud in the sky.

Then God made breakfast, and we set off for Mount Horeb for forty days. Forty is apparently the number of days for God's boot camp. Buckle up, Buttercups. Forty is a test. Sustained by God's breakfast of champions, Elijah walks across the desert for 960 hours.

We climb up the mountain of the Lord and into a cave. Finally, a chance to sit. Previously, I knew nothing of Mount Horeb. But now that we're here, I see it looks exactly like Mount Sinai. This is God's mountain—the mountain of the Ten Commandments. This cave looks like the cleft Moses crouched in. It's hard to see in the dim light, but I examine the rock walls, halfway expecting to see graffiti declaring, "Mo was here."

In the dark, God speaks. "Elijah. What are you doing here?"

Yeah, Elijah. What are we doing here? Seriously, dude. What does God have to do to convince you of his power, his strength, or his care? This is a strange time for a crisis of faith.

The forty-day jaunt across the desert hasn't changed Elijah's mind. He wants out. And he tells God in plain words. Suddenly, I'm aware of two things. First, Elijah isn't freaked out that the God of the universe is speaking with him. Second, amid overwhelming fear and discouragement, Elijah leans into God.

No wonder God picked this guy. He's courageous. Even when terrified, exhausted, and praying for death's relief, he takes his issue to God.

And God answers. "Be ready, Elijah. You want to see me? Then see me."

I know what's about to happen because I've read this before. But Elijah waits in the cave, every muscle tensed.

Suddenly, the cave is assaulted by a wind so powerful it crushes stone. Petrified, I want to run away, but my legs are paralyzed with fear. I press into the solid cave wall. It doesn't even vibrate, but the pounding of boulders against the outer walls is deafening. The ground billows like the sea. Off balance, I lean back against the rock to keep from falling. Elijah remains planted near the opening of the cave. And then a blast of heat fills the air as fire blazes across the mountain. It licks up the grass, the dirt, the stones. I recognize this fire.

My mouth works to form the trembling words. "You are God. You are God." It's all I can say, all I can think.

And then—a whisper. I strain to hear but can't make out words. This private message is for God's prophet. Then Elijah springs into action. Flinging his coat over his head, he heads out to stand before his God.

And suddenly, I'm filled with understanding. God didn't fail Elijah. Elijah's agenda failed Elijah.

My mind flashes back to Elijah's triumphal race against the chariots into Jezreel. He runs into the city, expecting this to be a pivotal moment. The tide has turned—God has won. The people will overthrow their horrific leadership and turn again to the ways of the Lord. We were witness to God's power on the mountain, right? All the people fell before him. This is the next logical step.

Elijah's a smart and savvy rebel. There's a sizable price on his head, and no way would he run into the middle of town unless he thought God would bring a victorious end to all the injustice.

But turns out it's business as usual in the city. The citizens finally have the water they need to get on with their lives. Jezebel is powerful as ever, except now the dragon lady is royally ticked off that Elijah killed all her pet prophets.

And Elijah thinks, "Wait, what? God, where are you? This isn't how it's supposed to go."

Somewhere during the chariot race, Elijah ran ahead of God.

And I was reminded of the many times I'd felt disappointed by God. Divorce, cancer, suffering. When I prayed during those times, my thoughts always betrayed me. "Where are you, God? How could you let this happen?"

When God failed to intervene in a way I could see—when prayer hung in the sky without an answer to record in my journal—I perceived letdown.

When I approached God, I planned our conversation in ways that made sense to my humanity. I expected God to be reasonable. I created correlations like, "God is loving, so he will relieve this suffering," or "God is just, so he will bring about the justice I desire." And when the situation went south, I felt betrayed.

Betrayal kills trust. And when trust dies, faith fails.

And that's why I needed to learn to be silent—to wait and listen before him.

God responds to Elijah: "My plan is not your plan. But My plan is always working."

When I feel betrayed by God, it isn't God who fails, but my limited understanding of a limitless being. I don't understand God. But really, do I even want to serve a God I can fully understand? Do I want a God who's small enough to fit into the plotted graph of my human prayer requests chart?

When a limitless being strikes a friendship with a limited being, there's a mismatch.

It happened to Elijah. Even after all he learned, he ran ahead of God. In the cave, God reassures Elijah: "I am the Leader."

I wondered why God displayed his power in those ways. Why not simply whisper? Clearly, Elijah's listening. He just completed a prophet's version of the Ironman to get closer to God. And then I was reminded of all the story circles with Jesus and his disciples. It's not the power that convinces—it's a personal interaction with God that changes the person. Jesus was raised from the dead. If that amount of power doesn't convince a person, then *no* amount of power will.

Elijah got to witness some of the most bold, amazing displays of God's power. But God said, "Kiddo, it ain't the razzle-dazzle that sustains you. It's my voice. My words. *Me*."

It was personal interaction with God that would change me. No amount of knowledge or reading or doing good things would change me—just space and time alone with God would produce change. A finite creation responding to its infinite Creator.

The Duplicator version of Christian living is anemic. Every week we plod off to church to hear a sermon. Every day we dutifully read the devotional and strategically selected Bible verses. But listening to people talk about God, or reading books that explain God, is not *being with God*. Even when I filled myself with worthy things—worship music and C. S. Lewis—it was all secondary input. Using a translator app just isn't the same as speaking the language.

God was waiting for me to sit with him. Just him.

I gotta say, this trip with Elijah was quite illuminating.

No wonder my prayer life was so frustrating. Although I had made progress in my understanding of the God or *not* God relationship, it hadn't filtered down into my stillness. At my deepest level, I was afraid to let God be God. But in the cleft of the mountain, I was reassured. Sitting alone with God is not a strategy session to make human sense of anything. It's a recalibration. It's not God's strength I believe in—it's God himself.

This was my introduction into experiencing joy that's unrelated to circumstances. Sitting without an agenda before the Maker of the universe, waiting on him to keep his promises, and knowing that he will—in his way and in his time. God's ways are more wonderful than human reason can fathom. This way of relating—limited being in the presence of limitless God—clips the invisible threads of human logic, which dictate that joy must be related to circumstance. I trust in God, not my understanding of God's response or perceived lack of response. Thus, my confidence is unshaken.

I left Elijah there on the mountain, listening to the still, small voice. I walked slowly down the path and into my bedroom. Pulling the covers up to my chin, I stared at the ceiling.

I decided to call God.

Ring, ring. Hello, God? I want to learn how to do that. I want to learn how to be still and know you are God.

"If you want to see me, then see me."

It was a call to action. I'd thought that waiting on God was passive, but God called me to see him—to look for him in every place and in every moment. And something shifted. I wasn't looking for God's answer to my prayers, my needs, and my requests anymore. I was looking for God.

Small moments are ideal for hearing his voice. Turns out God's favorite method of movement is not on the mountaintop. It's in the carpool lane on a Tuesday. Freed from searching for God's adherence to my agenda, I began to find God everywhere. His agenda was vastly more intriguing, and the most joyful moments came bursting onto the scene at the oddest times.

I learned to sit in silence and solitude before my Creator. What about the static in my head? Well, it would make a good story to say it subsided, but it didn't. My brain is cluttered and chaotic and in huge need of the *Clean Sweep* crew. I did read books on how to accomplish these disciplines and discovered some great tips.

Most importantly, I threw time at the thing. It was the best advice from my research. Makes sense that if something is difficult, more practice is warranted. It's hard. Even now, as soon as I hit the silence button, the chaos in my head has a dance party. But then I walk through the dance floor and talk to God about it: "God, I'm not sure why I'm worrying right now about that friend at work. Is there something I should do about it, or should I keep moving forward?" Or, "God, I'm thinking about the color of my grandma's kitchen counter. Can you please help me focus?" Slowly, we move through the crowd and clear the room. And when the space is fairly empty, I focus on the fact that God is right there. It takes time and some consistency to feel the friendship of God. But I proceeded with an understanding that no one but myself could work through this with God.

Sitting silently before God is extraordinarily powerful. But right now you're reading the Duplicator version of it. You must discover this personally in order to truly get it.

On the perch of Mount Sinai, I discovered that spending time with the disciplines of silence and solitude is supremely beneficial in advancing the warrior life. Turns out it's not the visible manifestations of God's power that change us. It's not our behaviors or any amount of knowledge. It's the relationship—give and take, push and pull—with our Creator.

God calls all of us to the Church of Transmogrification.

CHAPTER 10

Slaveworld

The passion of Christianity comes from deliberately signing away my own rights and becoming a bondservant of Jesus Christ. Until I do that, I will not begin to be a saint.

—Oswald Chambers, *My Utmost for His Highest*

I LIKED HANGING OUT WITH ELIJAH. IT SATISFIED MY SOUL. IT also satisfied my desire for God to show a vestige of his power—for every knee to bow—and for the world to finally acknowledge that God is the only way. This craving for justice is common to all humans. Even those who don't know God crave his justice. We want the happy ending that comes when good conquers evil.

Unfortunately, God doesn't blow off the tops of mountains very often.

Most of life involves doing mundane and insignificant things over and over. The life of the warrior involves infinitely more small moments than mountaintop experiences.

All of us with attentional deficits just sighed in despair.

It's easy to find aspects of daily life meaningless, like matching socks or scrubbing the sink, because it's so common. And repetitive. And *boring*. I never wake up thinking, "Oh my word! It's laundry day. I've been waiting for this day all week. Let's get started!" I'm not alone. Many of us find daily behaviors monotonous or even downright dreary.

For example, we don't want to see the small stuff in movies. Don't show me someone waiting for the bus or heating up the Easy Mac or running to the store to buy tampons. If the director does include the small stuff, it's sped up and truncated into a montage. Cue the music. Rolling out cookie dough with adorable flour smear on cheek. Delivering perfectly baked cookies to a delighted, quilt-clad family member. But they don't show the frustration over flour spills or the face one makes when they run to Walmart for butter because no one added it to the blessed grocery list. In my own life, please cut the footage of my colorful language when I burn my finger because I can't find an oven mitt. Unless, of course, I'm looking for a dishtowel, and then all we have are twenty-nine oven mitts.

When it comes to editing for our entertainment, the first thing we cut is reality.

But here's what warrior training illuminated. Reality is where God exists. Christianity is not wish fulfillment—it's reality management. God's blue ribbons are awarded most often in the seemingly insignificant tasks of life. Contrary to our human preprogramming that seeks validation through big accomplishments, God brings validation into small, broken moments with small, broken people. This is how we can experience true joy, regardless of circumstance.

I was motivated by joy. I wanted to understand what it really is and to experience it in real time. Joy seemed to be an *indicator species.* It was like the spotted owl of Romans Eight.

Let me explain. It's sometimes difficult to calibrate the health of a forest. There are millions of variables. But if the spotted owl disappears, something is definitely amiss. One or more of the subsystems is malfunctioning, and the balance is off. So forest management teams make changes and tinker with the subsystems. When the spotted owl returns, assumptions are made about the health of the environment. The forest is on the mend.

When joy exists, we can make assumptions that the subsystems of faith are alive and kicking. Joy is an indicator that I'm resting in my status as *not* God. So if I experience long periods of time without joy, something must be wrong in the kingdom of my heart.

Joy is a feeling. It's an emotional response to a preceding thought or event. Joy isn't something under my control. I can't command myself to feel joyful, although I have certainly tried. Every single time we attempt family photos, someone isn't having a good day. But considering the family Christmas card would look weird without one of our members, I force my grumpy progeny to put on a happy face. I enhance the message with every known threat to parenting. But it's clear to anyone who actually views the picture that putting on a happy face is vastly different from genuine feeling.

Joy isn't easy to understand. It often gets mixed up with the word *happiness*, which is like joy's loud and unpredictable cousin. Happiness is humanly logical. When someone looks happy, and you ask that person why they're happy, they can usually answer. "This lady agreed to marry me" or "I found ten bucks." Happiness has a lot to do with wish fulfillment. When we get something we want, especially if we've wanted it for a long time, we feel happy. But happiness is fickle and fleeting. When we do get what we want, it only satisfies us for so long—ask any kid at three o'clock on Christmas Day. Happiness is based on wish fulfillment, and it's transient at best.

We mix up the definitions of happiness and joy often, and even use the words interchangeably. But this doesn't make much sense. Paul says Jesus endured the cross "for the joy set before him." Clearly, something bigger than happiness was in play there. Jesus wasn't looking forward to getting the job done simply so it wasn't hanging over his head. He was gazing upon beloved children.

Because we intermix happiness and joy, some Christ-followers disregard the fact that joy is an emotion, and emotions must be *felt*. As a kid, my Sunday school teachers taught me to sing "I've got the joy, joy, joy, joy down in my heart." The problem is that as I stared into their faces, it was clear some of them hadn't experienced joy since Nixon was in office.

One morning, while reciting my verse in the Little Lamb's class, I remember asking Mrs. Krebbs how I could know I was feeling the joy of the Lord. She looked at me—startled—and then responded, "The joy of the Lord is something you *have*, not something you *feel*."

Spoiler alert—Mrs. Krebbs was wrong.

So I was confused about the joy of the Lord for years. How could you *have* joy but not *feel* joy? Little Hollylu's brain shoved it into the *too confusing to mess with* category, along with the doctrine of the Trinity and the mystery of God working all things together for good, even heinous crimes against humanity.

But I wasn't a kid now. Knock, knock. Mrs. Krebbs? I'm pretty sure you and John Piper wouldn't be able to run a three-legged race. John Piper has written entire books on the error of your thinking. In fact, he coined the scandalous phrase *Christian Hedonism* to describe the massive role joy plays in the Christian life—and in all of creation—and God's purposes within joy: "God is most glorified in us when we are most satisfied in him."[17]

Contrary to many church lessons during my formative years, God is not anti–good feelings. Joy isn't a hypothetical theory—it's a real thing. And this is how you know if you have it—you *feel* it.

However, we often misidentify the source of joy. When good things happen, we feel good. No surprise there, because anyone can feel happy when the chips are falling the right way. But what about when the train goes off the rails? Where is joy then? The apostle Paul said all kinds of far-out stuff about the source of his joy: "In all our troubles my joy knows no bounds" (2 Corinthians 7:4).

Umm. Really?

To actually feel joy when experiencing pain—that's a tough row to hoe. It's massively difficult. And with seemingly confusing verses like this in the Bible, it's much easier to embrace the doctrine of Krebbs. The joy of the Lord must be something we can have without actually feeling it.

Whenever I try to make God's promises fit my experience—when the experience doesn't match the promise—it's a hard sell.

Joy isn't optional. I must fight for it.

---

17 John Piper, *Desiring God* (Sisters, OR: Multinomah Books, 1996), 417.

Experiencing joy in the midst of pain is an indicator of living inside Romans Eight and that the subsystems of faith are alive. So I launched a quest for spiritual health. And since it's hard to grasp the complexity of all the subsystems involved in spiritual health, I decided to view joy as my spotted owl.

My premise was to keep embracing spiritual disciplines with the hope that volitional behaviors would influence my habitual self to move toward Jesus. More and more owls of joy would fly through the forest. And then I could assume—scientifically speaking—the subsystems of my faith were becoming healthy. Of course, I had to have an awesome moniker for this mission. *Code Name—Joy in Real Time.*

And now we circle the coffee cart back to the small moment conundrum. My life was generally not very interesting reading. In fact, entire years could be condensed into three-minute montages that involve driving around in a minivan. While I had an internal desire to live big for God, I mostly separated the recycling from the garbage. On really exciting days, I swept dog hair out of the kitchen.

Warrior Training Night School continued with the voracious 3D Bible-reading sessions. I found myself frequently following the apostle Paul around. We got pretty used to each other—him with the run-on sentence and me with the million questions. I felt like a sheepdog harassing the peaceful tranquility of Scripture. What does that mean? How do you do that? No offense, but you don't have children. Let's try that verse while all the kids are down with the flu.

I loved Paul's letters. They had beauty and a certain flow. But reading Romans was like sitting through algebra. It was impossible to read more than a few verses without experiencing information overload. One night Paul was a little patronizing.

"I am using an example from everyday life because of your human limitations" (Romans 6:19).

Really, your Apostleship? Please go on.

"Just as you used to offer yourselves as slaves to impurity and to ever-increasing wickedness, so now offer yourselves as slaves to righteousness leading to holiness" (Romans 6:19).

Yes, I know. Slavery isn't an option. We only choose what—or whom—we serve.

Paul stood up and looked at me. "In what ways are you a bondservant?"

I laughed. Seriously? I live to serve. This whole house is one glorious opportunity to embrace my status as live-in maid.

Paul squinted at me. "Keep reading."

He always said that. And truly, the more I read Romans the easier it became to understand. At this rate, I should be ready to move out of primary class in another seventy-one years.

Slavery is a tricky subject. And it's particularly tricky in Romans because sometimes Paul refers to the institution of slavery while other times he uses slavery as a word picture. Clearly, in this situation Paul uses the concept of slavery to highlight the caliber of our allegiance. In chapter 6 of Romans, the slave is completely subservient: "But thanks be to God that, though you used to be slaves to sin, you have come to obey from your heart the pattern of teaching that has now claimed your allegiance" (v. 17). There he goes, referencing patterns. The subconscious mind, the habitual self.

The goal is to not only declare allegiance to God with my conscious mind but also to make my subconscious self a slave to righteousness. No pushback against God, just total slave brain.

Paul's dim eyes crinkled with a smile. I waited for my Hello Kitty sticker, which I now insisted upon receiving whenever we had a breakthrough. The Sparkle Flower Journal of Awesomeness was filling up. But I digress.

So if I can't tap directly into my subconscious self, how do I train myself to thirst after God, so much so that I do it without thinking? Dallas Willard says discipleship is "learning from him how to lead my life as he would lead my life if he were I."[18]

Discipleship is a big word. And I've admitted the word is associated with lots of previous failure. In church when I was a teenager,

18 Dallas Willard, *The Divine Conspiracy: Rediscovering Our Hidden Life in God* (New York: HarperOne, 2018), 312.

there was a big push to get everyone into discipleship groups. It was a great idea. However, the execution eliminated a lot of grace, and mostly I lied about my spiritual behaviors—a double sin—or avoided going to group. The word *discipleship* was intimidating. Instant psych-out. Perhaps you're the type of person who would never be intimidated by a word, and you might be wondering when I will mature. Please message me, and I'll connect you with my mother. When it comes to waiting for people to mature, she's a champ.

If I was going to move forward, it was time for some rebranding.

Welcome to Slaveworld.

Slaveworld involved embracing the life of a slave to righteousness by embracing spiritual disciplines. This was nothing like my previous failures in discipleship because I finally grasped my non-voting status in this club. I wasn't a helpful team member. I was an S-L-A-V-E. God is God. I am *not* God. This idea constantly streamed like a newsfeed across my thoughts.

The goal was to embrace subconscious behaviors on a conscious level. And the best way I found to do this was to work through the spiritual disciplines with the goal of applying them in daily life. *My* daily life.

There are many good books that explain the spiritual disciplines and how to apply them. This isn't one of those books. This is about how one woman fought for her blessing and, in doing so, found the kingdom of God was at hand. However, most authors agree that there's usually a corresponding discipline to apply to an identified weakness.

For me? I wanted relief from a nasty sin habit—my perpetual need to please people. Don't scoff. People pleasing is a dangerous, sycophantic behavior pattern. It robs vitality and clouds the heart. And most of us don't even realize how deeply we're ensnared.

I've already told you that I was born craving attention. I wanted credit, and I needed people to know I was a winner. This groove went deep. I sought the approval of the world like a drug addict stumbling out of the methadone clinic. A base, primal desire for human affirmation. It didn't matter as much what God thought of me, although

I did care. What really mattered was what other people thought of me. This isn't the sort of thing that Good Christians talk about. In fact, I usually cover it up because if people knew the truth, they might think poorly of me. Therefore, I'm caught in a spider web of closeted sin. And I'm not alone.

In her groundbreaking book, *The Disease to Please: Curing the People-Pleasing Syndrome*, psychologist Harriet Braiker describes how people pleasing disables women in the workplace. It's not necessarily about making other people happy—it's about controlling the perceptions of others. It's simply unacceptable to have someone upset with me. I must work to keep them and their perceptions satisfied, even at the expense of my needs or my family. And it often works. Taking care of people makes them feel good. And then I feel good. But like all addictive behaviors, people pleasing is a dead end.

> Holding on to conditional beliefs about how people should behave toward you because of all you do for them will only set you up to feel disappointment, anger, and resentment to people in particular as well as disillusionment about others in general.[19]

It's as if Harriet sits beside me on the bus.

This need for approval was really messing stuff up. My marriage, my parenting, my ability to experience joy. Although I couldn't fully explain it, I felt hostage to the opinions of others. I needed everyone to be pleased with my existence. The problem is, I'm incredibly opinionated and sure to annoy at least half a dozen people per day. And then I'd worry about them being annoyed. Not so much that I wanted to be silent, but enough that I had a hard time focusing on my husband at dinner.

My people-pleasing need was crippling. To cope, I wouldn't think about it. Mostly, I moved so fast and filled my schedule with so much that there wasn't room to breathe.

---

19 Harriet B. Braiker, *The Disease to Please* (New York: McGraw-Hill, 2001), 23.

The counterpunch to people pleasing appeared to be the spiritual discipline of secrecy. Secrecy is about remaining anonymous. The premise behind the behavior is to do things for God and God alone. No credit. You may be thinking of anonymous donations or quietly decorating a Christmas tree and buying presents for an under-resourced family. But we're working in the realm of my real life. Not a lot of spare cash, and not too many Christmas-tree-ninja missions in June. Remember, my life—and perhaps yours as well—is mostly filled with monotonous behavior. Not a problem. God is okay with minutiae. If you don't believe me, read Leviticus.

One morning, I was running out of the house when I noticed all the family shoes had migrated into the hallway. Sweet baby Moses. Tripping over the shoes was some sort of maternal kryptonite.

And I heard a small voice say, "Why don't you put them away? In secret."

Are you kidding me? This is completely inappropriate. These people need to learn to put their shoes away. Someday I'll be eighty years old, visiting my offspring, and I'll topple over the shoes in the hallway and bust a hip. My job is to teach them responsibility and thus avoid future orthopedic consequences.

The voice stated, "You are my bondservant."

I paused. Then sighed. I will do this because I love you. I'm not doing this for them.

"I do not despise small beginnings."

So I put the shoes away. And no one besides God noticed. I'm not very patient. I don't want to wait for a heavenly reward—I prefer instant acknowledgment. At this rate, my crown in heaven is as bare as a baby's bottom.

Please note: When working on secrecy, serving your own children is a perfect training ground. If you're waiting for approval or gracious thankfulness from your peeps, let us know so we can send a search party to find your skeletal remains.

The next morning, the shoes were strewn across the hallway like manna from heaven.

"Are you my bondservant?"

Yes, I am. But the kids must learn to do this. How will they go to college? How will they survive marriage? Shoe management is essential to communal living. It's my job to teach them these things.

Instantly, my mind flooded with a million moments of fighting over the shoes. Mostly me arguing. My voice yelling, my hands waving, my mouth frothing, while the kids just stood there looking at me with their blank little faces. Apparently, me yelling about shoes is part of life in this house.

Fine. I'll put the shoes away. But this doesn't feel right. I'd rather be decorating a Christmas tree.

Every morning the shoes appeared, more reliably than taxes. And every morning I argued with God over the merits of doing someone else's work. Some mornings, I refused my status as bondservant. I would march the little delinquents into the house and stand glowering over them while shoe sanity was restored. But that didn't feel right either.

Eventually, I did get pretty used to it. I'd pass those shoes—mingling in the hallway like groupies at a concert—and shout in my head, "Yes, I am a bondservant!" while tossing the shoes into the baskets as if trying to set a land speed record. Occasionally, I mentioned the shoes in my Sparkle Flower Journal of Awesomeness. "Note—Still picking up the shoes. Because God asked. I still don't want to pick up the shoes. No one in this family has remotely noticed the shoes magically appearing in the right spot. Thanks for nothing, Dallas Willard."

A full six months went by. Life with kids is similar to dog years. Six months is equivalent to three decades. I was cleaning out Teddy's backpack when I unfolded a crumpled-up drawing. Under a picture of a blue house—clearly our house—he had written in his spidery handwriting, "My mom loves me because she makes me laugh and cleans the house even when the vacuum is broken." Lopsided hearts floated in the sky next to a bright sunshine.

I fixated on the "making him laugh" part because generally I was the bad cop parent. The nagging, uptight, get-your-booty-in-bed-before-I-have-a-meltdown parent.

But a subtle shift occurred so gradually that it was almost imperceptible. As I picked up the shoes again and again, I somehow stopped seeing them as a sign of defiance or my failure as a parent. I simply saw them as a sign of life with children. And mornings became way less stressful. We rushed like always, but we were more of a team. They were my children. My sheep. See, they still need me to pick up the shoes. Somewhere along the way, it became a privilege to serve these little gifts from God.

I stood with his drawing in my hands for a long, long time. I stared at the blue house with hearts in the sky. I wondered why the shoes on the floor had bothered me so much. Once upon a time, we'd started every morning with shoe shaming. Frustrated by my lack of acknowledgment, I demanded my rights. Why should I be the one to pick up the shoes? But now I wondered, Why *shouldn't* I pick up the shoes? Such a small gift to give.

And in that moment, joy beyond human reason flooded my soul. What had changed? The amount of thankless work that equals mothering? No. My status in the world at large? No. Would the shoes now put themselves away? Not a chance. But here was God's blue ribbon. And it involved my most cherished son. Nothing—absolutely nothing—could top this moment of joy.

How did I change? I'm not sure how, but God worked his magic somewhere in me. Obedience was key and so was love. Time helped, too, like a flowing river that wears stones smooth. If you and I spoke at the beginning of the experiment, I could've provided a slideshow presentation highlighting all the reasons putting away my kids' shoes was an ineffectual and pointless exercise in my journey of being a loving mom. I wasn't just indifferent to the idea—I was totally opposed to it. But then God changed my heart. He worked at a level I couldn't access on my own, and the softening reaped benefits all over the place with the people I cared about most.

It wasn't a straight line, but it was the absolute starting point for my journey of becoming free from people pleasing. I'm not finished yet, but I'm certainly not who I used to be. The conscious behavior of throwing shoes into baskets tapped into my subconscious habit of claiming my rights in the shoe department. As I constantly surrendered this right, my thinking began to change, and I no longer struggled with the decision to put the shoes away. I just did it.

The prospect of the righteous is joy.

For years I tried to make Christ following into a wish-fulfillment deal. But really, Christ following is reality management. Because *this* moment is the only place where God and I can interact. Reality is both brutal and breathtaking. It's *real.* And so is God.

That night I taped Teddy's drawing into the Sparkle Flower Journal of Awesomeness right next to my Hello Kitty stickers. Under the heading *Code Name—Joy in Real Time*, I wrote, "We're definitely on the right track. New goal—become chief citizen of Slaveworld."

CHAPTER 11

Embracing Hudson

An adventure is only an inconvenience rightly considered. An inconvenience is only an adventure wrongly considered.

—G. K. Chesterton, *On Running After One's Hat, All Things Considered*

HAVE YOU HEARD OF THE AWESOME TELEVISION SHOW CALLED *Man vs. Wild*? It wouldn't normally be my first choice—what with six seasons of *The Love Boat*—but since television is my main method of bonding, I watched it with my son. The show features Edward Grylls—rebranded as Bear Grylls—who gets dropped off in a forsaken area of the planet and must survive while navigating back to civilization.

Episode after episode, the man thwacks, splashes, and literally crawls his way back to humanity. This is the best analogy I could think of for warrior training. In fact, I created my own survivalist show in my head called *Ezer vs. Reality*. The plane would fly into Scripture, drop me off in the middle of ancient somewhere, and then I would use all my warrior tools to find my way back to real life.

It wasn't enough to want to change or to wish that Scripture would magically ring true in the postmodern age. I had to beat through the bushes. Cross streams. Hack firewood with machetes until God's soul-sustaining Word flowed into real time. Slow work indeed. All the worldly demands of working, living, and going on coffee runs made holy trailblazing difficult.

But I discovered that using spiritual disciplines was helpful in the field. There always seemed to be a discipline that made a reasonable companion for the portion of Scripture where I camped. For example, practicing secrecy coincided well with studying King Saul, poster child for codependence. I tried to alternate between the disciplines of retreat and advance because too much of any one discipline felt frustrating. I'd write notes in my journal and award myself stickers for bravery. Or good effort. Or for not calling anyone an *ass* in over a week.

Small steps, people.

When the plane dropped me off in a new part of Scripture, I'd read it voraciously. Again and again. It used to feel odd, but by now I'd decided normal was overrated and out of reach. Might as well just embrace the weird. I'd set up my tent inside the passage and try to get to know all the key players. Trotting along beside the biblical characters, I'd interview them like a roving reporter. I'd feel the grass, climb the tree, and see what changed from different vantage points. Gathering up all the information, I summarized my discovery like a scientist taking field notes. "Observation: Saul only spares his son Jonathan because his men demand it. He needed to please his men more than anything else. People pleasing is deadly." Then I'd test the discovery with other passages of Scripture. And with whatever remaining time I could carve out, I looked for insight from authors who wrote about their own adventures in these passages.

I was rolling along. With every new episode of *Ezer vs. Reality*, I'd fight for my blessing and wrestle for my joy. Not against God, but against my Romans Seven Self. She wasn't going anywhere without some serious mortification.

I was working through the Beatitudes. Can we all agree the Beatitudes are like lifting a bar of solid gold? Hey, ooh, shiny. Let me pick this up. Wait—what? This thing weighs a million pounds. How do you actually lift it? One day, I was wondering about the humility of spirit. Here is a shiny thing practically impossible to lift. Generally, humility is something we think everyone else should be working on. In the world, in the workplace, and even at home, we worry about someone taking advantage of us. And since I tend toward people pleasing, it's tough for me to know when to stop or when to say no. So if I'm working on humility and serving others, that means saying *yes* without focusing on glory or credit.

Excuse me, Mr. Grylls. I need a bigger machete.

My workplace was confusing. For many years I had a work self and a home self—and come to think of it, I had a church self too. That's a lot of selves. It's difficult to manage, especially for us unorganized types. So I kept the compartments sealed tight. No cross contamination. My coworkers didn't know my home self, and my family didn't know my work self. It was easier this way because that Christian stuff was hard enough to do with my loving family. Imagine turning the other cheek in the workplace. Cue the hearty laughter.

But God was calling me to be *one* person. His bondservant. All the other selves had to be reined in and consolidated into the ezer. This was intimidating mainly because I was afraid of people being unhappy with me.

So back to the Beatitudes. How was I going to keep the boundary with the people-pleasing sin while working on humility? Apparently, the plane dumped me off in the fire swamp.

One morning I was sitting with God looking at trees. It was smack in the middle of a Northwest fall, and the foliage was stunning. I asked him how I was going to be humble for reals—having already graduated from the master class of false humility—but also not overdo it and then get mad at everyone?

"Make the path straight."

Wait a sec. Have you seen my survival show? Everything I'm doing is focused on finding the connection between what I know and what I do. It's hard to find a straight path when it's all virgin territory.

For the rest of the day, I meditated on this verse: "'Make level paths for your feet,' so that the lame may not be disabled, but rather healed" (Hebrews 12:13). How could I make the path straight? Well, I suppose I could use the Plan-Do-Review strategy.

I work with many people who have unique brains and unusual nervous systems. The goal is to work *with* the nervous system, not against it. Working against the nervous system is like swimming upstream. It's possible, but why? A more effective strategy for task completion is to make a plan, do it, and then review how it went to see if any changes need to be made. As with most effective strategies, it's super simple.

Perhaps I could make a plan for implementing my humility goals into real life. This would cut down on my nightly journaling. Until now, I would mostly write experientially about my day. I'd look for evidence of growth or lack of growth. The journal was reactive rather than proactive. Writing out a plan might help focus my efforts so I'd be slower to bail out when things got hard.

But I didn't want to ruin this adventure with God. Goal setting was something that didn't fit in well with my slapdash personality. I also worried about overly focusing on accomplishments and slipping back into my Good Christian ways. This was definitely a risky proposition. I decided to make it a one-time deal and abandon it quickly if I felt like it was pulling me off course. What happens in the fire swamp stays in the fire swamp.

Goal setting is an art form, and I've learned that spending time in serious goal development is always worth it. The goal should be written so specifically that you can answer the question "Did I reach my goal?" with a thumbs-up or a thumbs-down.

But this brought up more mental thickets. How do you write a goal about humility? How do you measure a beatitude? I'm not sure—I guess you just try. I came up with this: "At Tuesday's staff meeting, I'll wait for someone to ask my opinion before I speak up." Very specific and answerable with a yes or no. I recorded my goal and waited for Tuesday, arming myself with some heavy hitters in Proverbs about the folly of the tongue. I reviewed my verses several times a day. I created a mental picture of myself not talking. Scarce source material. When Tuesday arrived, I strapped on the wilderness pack and thwacked my way to the staff room.

I sat down with a pleasant smile on my face. We ran through the agenda, and about thirty minutes in, someone asked for my opinion. So I gave it. Goal accomplished!

Two coworkers asked if I was sick. Apparently, my lack of talking was a serious departure from baseline behavior. My boss even noted that we finished early. I smiled and felt a little pleased with myself in a very humble way. I couldn't wait to get home and write this victory up, baby.

And then it hit me. I just *knew*. God expected this to be my new status quo. The picking up shoes thing all over again.

So I geared up. Collected my verses, grabbed my machete, and hacked across Scripture and into my workplace. Tuesday was a victorious trial day. But time went on and various important topics came up, and when no one asked my opinion, I became frustrated. I must claim the right to express my most excellent and obviously correct thoughts. These people needed me.

I'd wrestle back to God, and he'd ask, "Are you my bondservant?" Well, yes. But I'm not my boss's bondservant, and I'm certainly not my coworker's bondservant. They aren't even appreciating any of this. It's like no one notices.

And then I stopped in the middle of my mental rant. *Oh.*

The Beatitudes. This was the first time I'd wrestled with them in real life. I'd always logically assented that the Beatitudes were otherworldly amazing and counter to human nature. I'd mentally note that it sure would be awesome if we lived more like that and then move on, believing it was close to impossible to do it. But here I was, bashing through the jungle between the fifth chapter of Matthew and my staff room, and I felt like running to the front of the church on Sunday morning shouting, "Have you guys tried this stuff? Like, for real? I'm dying here."

Until I started setting goals and reporting how I actually did, I didn't know where my particular sticking points were in Slaveworld. But I sure knew now. And I was discovering more every day. The hard spots were filling up the new Sparkle Eiffel Tower Journal—I had a new journal because I'd actually filled my entire old one. Can we take a moment to acknowledge this colossal achievement? Thank you, carry on—and when enough hard spots piled up, I'd use that to guide my next drop-off point in Scripture.

Let me back the bus up for a second. The goal was simply an awareness indicator or a measuring tool. Being silent in staff meetings wouldn't make me a humble person. I could've spoken quite humbly in the staff meeting and pleased God with my words. The point is this: spiritual discipline is an exercise. It's a process designed to give God access to the deeper, subconscious layers of the heart. We do stuff with the thinking part of our brains as a means of allowing God to do stuff with the autopilot system. So basically, setting goals provided me with a way to focus on bridging the gap between what I believed and how I lived.

Here's what I learned. My goals needed to be very, very small. Baby changes. I needed to target less important scenarios or scenarios where I had little emotional investment. This was just practice. Running laps. It wasn't the game. If I put myself on the spot when the stakes were high, I was more likely to fight against it. It was one thing not to speak up at a weekly staff meeting but another thing entirely not to speak up at my annual review.

I also let the goals flex and change. They were *my* goals, selected by me. They were tools. So over time, my staff meeting goal morphed into first allowing one or two people to speak before I spoke. I focused on listening carefully and not interrupting. I would often pause to ask God if he wanted me to speak up before I opened my mouth.

I also had to attach the goal to Scripture, preferably related to my current reading jag. I needed to know that God was shaping my path and making it straight. Once I got used to the rhythm, I had goals all over the place, in every environment. It was fun. In the coffee line, my goal was not to rush and to let anyone racing for the line go ahead of me. I did this in traffic too. When people cut me off or zoomed into my lane, I'd try to use it as a lesson in humility. If I felt anger, I asked

God why I was angry. Why do I care about a few feet of pavement? I am a bondservant. Bondservants don't have rights in the turning lane.

Granted, these were small-potatoes moments. Shaving a few seconds off the commute isn't truly important. But the posture of humility started coming to my aid when the stakes were higher. When my boss failed to mention my success at a meeting but praised others for smaller accomplishments, I felt my heart say, "What do I care? A bondservant doesn't have rights in the staff room." When we vacationed and one family member dominated the agenda, my heart responded, "What do I care? A bondservant doesn't have rights on vacation. A bondservant is just happy to be *on* vacation."

One night I was reflecting on these moments, and I had a terrifying thought.

Ring, ring. Umm, God? Am I turning into Hudson Taylor?

Not claiming my rights every waking second was foreign to my nature, but I was actually doing it. And it all started by not speaking in the staff room.

And *this* is the crazy, inside-out way of Jesus. To gain your life, you must lose it.

It's about understanding the nature of freedom. Best I can figure, there seem to be different levels of freedom. There are personal freedoms and experiential freedoms. And sometimes you can't have both. For example, the Olympic figure-skating champion has given up many personal freedoms in favor of early bedtimes and early morning alarms and clean eating. She gives up the right to go to parties or hang out at the mall—does anyone hang out at the mall anymore?—but by enslaving herself to figure skating, she gains an experiential freedom that the rest of us can't obtain. She flies across the ice without much thought. Her body is able to twist and jump and express beauty. Her slavery has made her free on a different—and arguably better—level.

The deeper we enslave ourselves in the pursuit of Jesus, the more alive in Christ we become. Unfortunately, it doesn't make sense from the bottom. Romans Seven will never understand Romans Eight.

Here's the deal with functional goal setting. It's a helpful tool. There's all kinds of research that proves when we write down goals, we're much more likely to achieve them. Why does writing help? It takes the goal out of the thinking phase and moves it closer to the action phase. Now you have both visual and physical memory of writing the goal, which makes it more likely to register and remain longer in your conscious thought. It's just good brain science.

When Harold Hill rolls into River City in the musical *The Music Man*, he's a huckster looking for vulnerable townspeople to fleece. He convinces the good citizens to fund a marching band to save local teens from moral depravity. Although Harold Hill can't play a note himself, he talks a big talk and convinces his pupils they only need The Think System to learn their instrument. The Think System involves concentrating really hard while listening to Beethoven's *Minuet in G* without actually playing the instrument.

The Music Man is a comedy, and we laugh at the notion of mastering something by simply thinking about it. But it appears I was using The Think System with the Beatitudes for years. I forgot—and many in the church have forgotten—that grace is free but righteousness is work. The only way to get the transformation we all claim to want is to show up, accept the assignment, fall on grace, and do it all over again tomorrow. The Christ-following life is filled with challenge. Risk, failure, victory.

Before I started goal setting with God, we still moved forward, but it was slow and rather willy-nilly. Goal setting was the rudder I needed to go faster and further with every assignment. And when really hard things came up, God gently led me toward the straight path.

Now let me assure you, lest lightning strike, that there were a lot of stalled moments, fussing, and complaining. Lame as it was to do so, I argued with God about the nature of my slavery. Transitioning to Slaveworld is tough, and it takes time and copious amounts of effort. Occasionally, I went backward, losing some hard-earned territory, and I'd grow discouraged. But God never failed. Somehow between my survival-show mentality and crazy assignments, some serious change was happening. The land of Eight was here. As my status in Slaveworld became more familiar, my confidence in God grew. He is God; I am *not* God. Thus, I'm all kinds of free.

If you live long enough, any forward momentum with God will be seriously tested. The rain falls on the evil and righteous alike. And cancer doesn't care who you are.

When my father-in-law was diagnosed, we rallied the troops. We pulled together as a family and prayed and waited on God. And we buried our dad thirteen months later.

It devastated me. It affected my marriage, my parenting, my friendships. My journals lay on the shelf. They now seemed trite, with their fake jewels and purple feathers. I stared at the cat-shaped stickers. How juvenile. None of this was a game. What was I doing?

I didn't ask God where he was. I knew he was with us. I didn't ask, "Why cancer?" I was a bondservant, with no right to assume God would answer my prayers the way I wanted. But I was heartbroken. I circled the wagons, taking care of my family and myself. I moved slowly and sat with grief.

This verified that significant progress had been made. But deep inside, I felt a terrible fear bubbling to the surface. What if my husband or one of my kids were next? Would I hate you, God? Would I despise you? It would be impossibly difficult to lose one of them, but I couldn't survive losing *you*.

And heaven was silent.

I wandered around aimlessly in Scripture. It comforted me a little, but I was tired and freshly overwhelmed with the realization that I didn't want to be a bondservant. All the changes so far indicated that someday I would morph into a person who could stand in the face of earth-shattering pain and say, "It is well with my soul." And I didn't want that. I didn't want to be okay with that.

How do you argue with God about pain and suffering? Where do you go with those questions?

I opened my Sparkle Flower Journal of Awesomeness and read through my discoveries. In some places, my handwriting was messy with excitement. I could hear my own breathless voice. "God is God. I am *not* God." Stomping through Scripture with my journal at the ready had been a wild, exciting adventure.

But now? My heart ached. I am *not* God. But I am in desperate pain.

There was no easy answer. But there *was* an answer. This is not the Real. The Real is to come. My father-in-law is already in the Real. There's no negotiating with God about his divinity. Freedom comes from embracing life as a bondservant.

I curled up in bed with my head on my Bible. I longed to be brave like Daniel. Defiant like David. But I felt small and trivial, like the plastic jewels on the outside of my journals. The room slowly grew dark. My husband was with his mom, and our kids were asleep. So I lay there in the stillness. The televisions and music were silenced. All I could hear was the quiet rumble of an occasional car passing by. Headlights briefly shone across the ceiling and then disappeared.

And suddenly, I was aware of the One who is closer than a brother. So close. I put my hand out. Perhaps he was close enough to touch. And all I could say is, "You are God. You are God."

Instantly, I was transported to the moment Dad's body was taken away from the house. I stood in the same spot where he used to stand by the window when he waved goodbye to us. And I waved and waved at the coroner's van until it rolled out of sight. My lips moved then, too, saying, "It's true. Now we know it's all true." Because in that moment, I had felt God say, "I have him."

I had forgotten this holy moment in the swirl of sorrow and chaos after death. Later I asked my sister-in-law if she remembered any of it. "I do remember you waving to the coroner's van like a lunatic. And you were talking to the window." My sister likes to tell the truth.

I don't know *how* God spoke to me in that moment. But he's a friend, so it makes perfect sense that he would.

And it occurred to me there in the dark. *This* is faith. *This* is hope. To be in the valley and know the high places exist—and to realize that someday it will all be put right. But we want the justice that Elijah craved, and we want it now. No one wants to wait.

I looked at my circle of biblical friends. They stood silently in the room. Ruth, Gideon, Bartimaeus. I whispered to the room of witnesses, "It seems like death won. I feel the sting." I couldn't look at Paul. I was afraid he would tell me to go read Romans. Instead, I gazed at David. The kid turned king, the one who ran after God.

David cleared his throat. He softly replied, "Truly, he is my rock and my salvation. He is my fortress. I will not be shaken. Trust in him at all times. Pour out your heart to him. For God is our refuge."

Yes. *Yes*. It's the only logical choice.

What hope is there for those separated from God? How do they survive these partings? It's unfathomable to me.

I used the phone even though God was sitting on the bed.

Ring, ring. Hello, God? My heart is broken. But I know it's all true. I know it. Forgive my weakness.

"Your weakness is where I do my best work. Hold on, baby girl. I'm here."

And my pain intermingled with such love and an overwhelming sense of rest. My friends slowly faded back into the dim light. God cradled my head in his lap. I watched the headlights flash across the ceiling while the Maker of the universe sang over me until I slept.

CHAPTER 12

Friends and Strangers

The person who loves their dream of community will destroy their community, but the person who loves those around them will create community.

—Dietrich Bonhoeffer, *Life Together: The Classic Exploration of Faith in Community*

TIME ROLLS ALONG, DOESN'T IT? SLOWLY, THE GRIEF EBBED A BIT, and small amounts of momentum returned. I continued setting goals. Simple goals. But progress was incremental. One day, as I tried to be humble about another driver's interesting means of pathfinding, I settled on this truth. It would be a lot easier to do this spiritual transformation thing if there weren't so many crummy people clogging up the place.

A pastor at church tells us, "We were made for community." But I always want to correct that statement. We were made for community with nice people. Jerks can go make their own community, preferably far, far from me.

Based on my in-depth and totally scientific observations, community works best if it stays shallow. Kiddie-pool shallow. What's the basis of this somewhat heretical opinion? Crowdfunding.

Crowdfunding is a platform for people to raise money on social media. Launched in 2010, GoFundMe now has one donation per second.[20] Per second. More than forty million people have used its

20 "Giving Report: To 2021, With Gratitude," GoFundMe, https://www.gofundme.com/c/gofundme-giving-report-2021.

simple app, wherein a person gives a short description of their need, attaches a photo, then posts it online and lets the dollars rack up. Most of the GoFundMe proposals are for people with true and overwhelming need, like a child who requires expensive surgery or a family who must rebuild their home after a hurricane. But too many are just regular people asking for a little help.

Asking ain't stealing.

Or is it?

According to online poll Ranker, the needs behind some crowd sourcing is a bit sketch.[21] A woman named Amira raised $6,000 toward her goal of playing professional golf in the LPGA. Never mind that she hadn't actually qualified to play at that level. Her proposal included tuition to LPGA Qualifying School in Mission Hills, California. After all, first things first.

In New York, Tabitha successfully raised over a thousand bucks to get a tattoo removed from her forehead. Logan, a teenager, raised more than $2,000 to pay off a speeding ticket. His original goal was $500, and he donated the additional funds to the military. An aspiring actress, Katelyn, raised over $1,200 to attend an acting workshop where she could possibly snag an agent. The list of requests is outrageous. I found requests to fund the following: a hedgehog; a gap year; tickets to see Phish for the fifty-second time, which was classified as "an absolute need"; attendance at a yoga-instructor school; a twenty-fifth birthday party; hats for a bald man; and extended vacation time in New York City.

I'm curious why this works so well. Clearly, one reason is that the global community of social media is much bigger than the village that any person works, plays, or drinks coffee in. But there's also the simplicity of ignorance. All the data points are condensed into one or two paragraphs, which are visually attached to a photo. It's interesting that we are willing to financially contribute to people we don't know. In fact, in Tabitha's case people within her own community—her

21 Ashley Reign, "The Dumbest GoFundMe Campaigns Ever," Ranker, https://www.ranker.com/list/dumb-gofundme-campaigns/ashley-reign.

friends and family—made comments insinuating that Tabitha might not be legit. "You had better use it for the tattoo this time," said one.

Hmm.

Interestingly, it appears we're more likely to help people we don't know, especially if they have a good picture. Research depressingly indicates that Americans are much more likely to contribute to a human-interest story—like Tabitha's tattoo—than an organization that publicizes statistics on program success—like the American Red Cross.[22] Please don't bother me with details. Show me the cute picture. As much as we fancy ourselves as thinking, logical people, we tend to lead with our emotions.

The fact that we are emotional creatures isn't breaking news. Emotions alert and inform our brains with necessary perspective. In 1946, March of Dimes printed a poster with before and after photos of polio survivor Donald Anderson.[23] Five-year-old Don appeared to walk bravely toward the camera under the words, "Your dimes did this for me." The campaign, which was wildly successful, launched the concept of the poster child. We connect and relate to a human face.

But peopling is hard to do. According to the Global Peace Index, fewer than ten countries are currently free from conflict.[24] Conflict in this context is defined as governmental authorities using weapons against citizens. Turns out once you get to know your community, those Beatitudes really stick in one's craw. It's much easier to love thy neighbor when the neighbor who disagrees with you is dead. Intimacy isn't considered a bonus for the average community participant. We might remember that Julie remodeled her kitchen last year, but now she's unemployed and needs help with grocery money. Pardon me while I raise an eyebrow. Or we might hear that Joe gambles in Vegas every

22 Ashley Reign, "The Dumbest GoFundMe Campaigns Ever," Ranker, https://www.ranker.com/list/dumb-gofundme-campaigns/ashley-reign

23 "In Memoriam: Donald Anderson, First Poster Child, 1940-2014," March of Dimes, https://www.marchofdimes.org/news/in-memoriam-donald-anderson-first-poster-child-1940-2014.aspx.

24 Global Peace Index Map, "The Most & Least Peaceful Countries," Vision of Humanity, https://www.visionofhumanity.org/maps/#/.

month, but his car recently broke down and he can't afford the repair. Now both eyebrows are raised.

It seems harder to extend grace to people who, in our opinion, haven't lived wisely. Grace is something we'd like to save for innocent victims. People who haven't contributed to the situation they're currently in. Doesn't justice dictate that you reap what you sow? Like Mama always said, "If you're gonna make that bed, you're gonna lie in it." People who don't live up to the community standard must learn from their mistakes.

The problem is that no one meets the community standard all the time. No one's perfect. This is the truth everyone knows but won't admit. So society runs on being known but not *too* known. It's best to keep the substandard parts of us hidden. Ever since humans stumbled out of the garden, our primary focus has been on keeping the ugly tucked in.

Shallow is as shallow does. The best type of community for people who actually want to remain in community is superficial, hiding one's baser parts and creating a connection that can coexist with isolation. Wait. How can a community develop from the guiding principle *never be the real you*? I don't know. Ask Mark Zuckerberg.

So if peopling is so hard, why do it? The answer is simple. God made us to function as team players. Without people connections, we shrivel up. In fact, without people, it's impossible to experience the full range of God's love: "No one has ever seen God; but if we love one another, God lives in us and his love is made complete in us" (1 John 4:12).

The problem is that we learned the rules to the game as designed by this world. Value comes first, then love. Strength is good, and weakness is bad. Try to find a strong community, then hide your weakness so you can stay.

Once we enter the kingdom, we find God's rules are exactly the opposite. Love is first, value second. Strength counts for little while weakness is an asset.

God calls us to exult in our weaknesses, as they are intersections for experiencing God. In the world, we're taught that value makes something worthy of love. But God reverses the order, insisting his love is what makes us valuable.

No wonder the Beatitudes are a punch in the gut. Like wearing a tutu to a cage fight, it's completely incongruous with the status quo. And by status quo, I mean *People* magazine.

And yet we're called to love as God loves, not as the world does. *Agape* love is the divine glue that holds community together. Agape—rhymes with frappe—describes the supernatural love of Jesus, a love that gives value to the receiver. It requires no predicating event. It's hard to understand that kind of unconditional love. But we see its reflection when a mother cares for her newborn at two o'clock in the morning. She's so tired she's forgotten her own name, but when she hears that cry, up she goes again. Agape is modeled by soldiers who serve and die for their country, far from home and often in places where their sacrifice goes unnoticed. We see agape when a police officer buys a pair of new shoes for a homeless man on a blustery winter night. He didn't know he was being recorded. He just wanted to help someone with cold feet.

Evidence of unconditional love goes viral all the time. As a species that has fallen from grace, we crave what was lost. Just not enough to push it from the category of what we *do* into the category of who we *are*. We're happy to rise to the occasion sometimes, but we don't want the standard to be raised. If unconditional love—or unconditional favor, service, or support—becomes the status quo, then how do we tell who's the greatest? It's fine for the big dog to occasionally be nice to the little dog. But if the big dog consistently treats the little dog like he *is* a big dog, we lose our ability to define greatness.

As my adventures in Slaveworld continued, it was clear that I had a long, long way to go in the area of community. I'm impatient, prone to grumpiness, and gigantically opinionated. I like to lead, and I definitely won't follow incompetent leaders. I prefer speed and find exactitude annoying. I don't like to be serious, and I usually laugh at entirely inappropriate times. Clearly, I'm not a walking billboard for God's kind of community.

But I'm not a quitter either. Life in Slaveworld was a powerful reformer. My experiences with God's agape love gave me hope. Armed with a new journal—a tad more sedate this time, covered in birds and fleur-de-lis—I ramped up the production schedule for *Ezer vs. Reality*.

Ring, ring. Hello, God? I'm ready. I want to be nice. I don't want to simply *act* nicely; I want to be a sponge that overflows with love, rather than sucking in status, power, acclaim, and blah blah.

"Make sure you know what you're doing."

Wait. What? Of course I don't know what I'm doing. Hence the prayer. I need you to teach me. I want to learn how to be the type of person who pulls everyone up. Points them to you, not just with my words but with my life.

"Mayhee was right."

What are you talking about? Mayhee? Graduate school Mayhee? Shouldn't you be referencing the apostle Paul or something?

"1 Corinthians 2:1; 1 Corinthians 1:18; 1 Corinthians 1:25; 1 Corinthians 1:21; 1 Corinthians 2:14; 1 Corinthians 1:27; 1 Corinthians 1:23."

Oh. Let me get a pen.

God was aiming me right up Dr. Mayhee's alley: "For since in the wisdom of God the world through its wisdom did not know him, God was pleased through the foolishness of what was preached to save those who believe" (1 Corinthians 1:21).

That sounds a lot like "Until you learn to unsee what is seen, you can't see the unseen."

Which boils down to this—we've got trouble right here in River City. We got trouble with a capital T, and that rhymes with P, and that stands for . . . paradigm.

Yep. The opposing paradigms of worldly community and God's type of community are so different, it's almost impossible for the two camps to even see each other. God was cautioning me to be aware. Aware that I'd be blind to the majority of the world grooves in my own heart. My understanding of community was developed deep inside. It wasn't going to be an easy connection between Scripture and life, mainly because my very interpretation of Scripture needed to be corrected. Please return to your seat and fasten your seatbelt. We'll be experiencing turbulence for the remainder of our flight.

I began by trying to write down the modus operandi for life in kingdom community.

We are called to be on a team. Every team member is an integral part of the team and should be treated as such. God is the Coach. The only Coach. Romans 12:4–5; Galatians 3:28–29.

The Coach leads by example, and we are to follow his lead (1 John 4:11). Team meetings encourage us and help us to not give up. Team meetings are not optional (Hebrews 10:24–25). The team plays together. Fighting with teammates is not acceptable. Be wary of people who try to divide the team (1 Corinthians 1:10; Romans 16:17). Teamwork is impossible without love. Love makes the team go (Colossians 3:14). The Holy Spirit makes it possible to live in unity on the team (1 Corinthians 12:13). The playbook is summarized in 1 Peter 3:8.

So far, so good. I wrote these guidelines down in the journal. Then I tried to write a goal. But what exactly was I trying to do? Who was the target environment—my family? My workplace? Maybe church? I tried for a few days to come up with a reasonable goal that pointed me in the general direction of God-style community.

The problem is that a goal about making community connections requires—wait for it—a community to connect with. I know. It's tough to be this smart. I needed another person who also wanted to work on connecting in God-style community.

Also, I do realize my husband and children are my first community. But since the rest of this book involves them, I thought I'd focus on my efforts to be in community with other women. Because women are so easy to figure out, said no one ever.

My first epiphany was that I needed a friend who met a few requirements. She had to live near me, desire to be a godly encouragement, and be amazingly tolerant of occasional diatribes, over use of stickers and glitter, and caffeine abuse. Now where to find her?

Cue the crickets.

It's not that I didn't have friends. I did. At work I had amazing, life-sustaining friends, but not godly friends. I also had godly friends, like my roommate from college and my bestie from graduate school, but they didn't live nearby.

Well, then.

Ring, ring. Hello, God? I need your help. I need to connect with a friend who wants to work with me to make both of us into better people. Please send her soon. Amen.

Maybe you've experienced this too. Finding friends as an adult can be surprisingly difficult. Once people have an established posse, it's hard to expand. Kids are much better at making friends. They build unity quickly, especially when they want to play.

One time my daughter was running all over the park with another girl I'd never met. She came up to me breathlessly, a new kid right behind her. "Don't worry, Mom," she said with glowing red cheeks. "This isn't a stranger." She patted the girl. "She's my friend."

"Oh." I smiled. "What's your friend's name?"

Anna wrinkled her face and then turned to the girl. "Friend, what's your name?" The friend wasn't remotely insulted. With a wide smile, she responded, "I'm Makayla." And away they went, so preoccupied with friend stuff that they barely had time for social niceties.

As adults, it's much harder. Typically, we are a bunch of false fronts, and no one knows what's in the building. It's against the rules to look needy. So if we need a friend, it's crazy hard to find other people needing a friend. Who thought up this plan? Oh, right. The enemy.

For a few months, I went to places I thought this godly woman might be hiding out. Bible study. Mothers of Preschoolers (MOPS) meetings. Starbucks. I beat a few bushes, sent out a few signals, tested the waters.

More crickets.

The women in these places appeared to already have the friends they needed. It felt like junior high all over again. Case in point: I once arrived early to a Bible study so I'd have more time to socialize with ladies. I sat at a table and started a conversation with a nice young woman. We actually laughed. It was the most promising nibble I'd had in weeks. And then, right before the study started, she scooped up her stuff. "Oh, my friends are here. Nice meeting you."

And I was left by myself at a table that seats eight. And instead of having the courage to invite myself over to the other table, I sat there with no one but Beth Moore for company. Beth Moore sat at my table. She loved me. She called me *beloved*.

Needless to say, the journal was filling up with false starts. I'd just have to be patient. *Gah*. Working on community and patience. It's like when a personal trainer has you work on two muscle groups at the same time—sneaky but effective. Months passed. It's not like I didn't have lots of other things to work on.

One day I watched my kids play at the park, marveling at how they developed new friendships that lasted until a mother called for her child. Smiling wanly, they'd watch their friend run off. With only seconds to regroup, they'd take a deep breath and gamely look around for a new friend. Park friendships required a lot of vulnerability. But apparently, park time was precious. If you wanted to play, you had to get on with it.

That night I returned to Matthew to watch the children climbing up onto Jesus's lap. He didn't stop them—he encouraged them. As I stood there, I was distracted by the disciples. They're restless. The kids are climbing all over Jesus and taking a huge chunk of the teacher's time. It's throwing off the schedule. I hear Phillip huffing as he checks his sundial. The disciples can tell Jesus is on the verge of something big. Important people have taken notice, and even the Pharisees are coming to Jesus. Attendance is way up, and now Jesus needs to focus. We're developing a brand here, and we need to be strategic. Peter wrinkles his nose. One of the babies needs a diaper change.

When the disciples block the way, Jesus rebukes them for using the wrong paradigm. This is the kingdom door, guys. You have to unsee what is seen.

What did I need to see? What did I need to unsee? Apparently, I was going to have to be more vulnerable when it came to looking for a friend. Then suddenly, a goal came to me. I would invite women out to pray. Not to drink coffee or exercise or shop. Just pray. I paused. This would not make me look cool. This might even damage whatever image I had.

But time is precious. If I wanted to make progress in Slaveworld, I'd have to get on with it.

And so I made a goal to invite at least one person to pray with me every week. The environment in which I found a woman—work, church, neighborhood—didn't matter. It didn't even matter if they said yes. The goal was to be vulnerable with my need.

Turns out *vulnerable* wasn't a strong enough word. It would've been far easier to pop a beer in the sanctuary. In fact, I would've rather drunk the entire pack. But every week, God provided someone to ask. I often clenched up at the last minute, stammering out my request. Sometimes I made an inappropriate amount of eye contact while waiting for their response, trying to read their facial expression. I felt the need to jump in quickly and judge them before they could judge me.

I started to rely on the fact that ladies would usually decline, what with having just been asked to pray with a stammering gargoyle. Occasionally—miraculously—the answer would be yes. Then I'd get all kinds of anxiety while waiting for our prayer date.

Every single one felt awkward. Uncomfortable. Weird.

Then one evening I was at a dinner party. I had dragged my husband there in an effort to find friends. The woman was not my type. She was overly pretty and physically fit. She was organized and ran a homeschool co-op. If you drew a Venn diagram of our overlapping interests, there would be two circles side by side. In other words, she was a perfect candidate for my request because there's no way she'd be interested in being my prayer partner.

I wasn't even nervous this time. I'd ask her, get a resounding no, and be off the hook for another week. So I asked my question and then stared at her face. She didn't respond quickly. She was thinking. Finally, she asked, "What would we pray about?"

No fair. You can't answer a question with a question. "Umm . . . stuff." I'm so eloquent. "Important stuff." I cleared my throat. "We'd pray about what we found important."

She stared back at me for a long time. Quit turning the tables, missy. "Would we do a Bible study?" she asked.

"No," I responded. That felt too emphatic. "I don't mind reading the Bible, but I mostly want to pray."

She kept staring at me, so I added, "I don't need to learn more. I need to do more of what I've learned."

Her eyes widened. Sheesh, is it getting warm in here? I sounded like an idiot. The fact that my husband was sitting at the table chatting with her husband kept me from running out of the room.

"I'll think about it."

Hmm. Is that a yes or a no? For data collection purposes.

This woman was unsettling. Eventually, my husband and I made our escape. I jumped into the car, and Mike laughed at the role reversal. "Burn rubber, honey," I said, buckling my seatbelt.

A few days later my phone rang. A very optimistic voice said, "I'm in." And because I'm not a person who remembers things for more than one day, I was confused. Who was this? What was she in for?

After stuttering for a minute, I discovered it was *her*. She wanted to get together and pray. Okay then. Between her incredibly full schedule of homeschooling, marathon training, leading MOPS, and cooking gourmet meals—and my incredibly full schedule of avoiding laundry and spending too much money at Walmart—we could meet at nine o'clock on Thursday evenings.

"Do you want to meet at Denny's?" I asked. I was suddenly afraid of being with a stranger, especially one who kickboxed for fun.

"No. I'll pick you up. We can just pray in the car."

It turns out this woman was God's version of dynamite. Our first night we talked. Sort of laughed uncomfortably. And then we bowed our heads to pray, and all of heaven stopped. The Maker of the universe bent down to listen, and I heard him whisper.

"Not a stranger. A friend."

We prayed in that car every week until she moved to Texas. She exploded through old, worn-out paradigms with glee. She pushed me. Challenged my assumptions. Questioned my motives. Her brain was massive and her heart so tender. I often left her presence somewhat troubled and needing to hash it out with God long after she'd left. It wasn't a walk in the park. It was better.

Alongside this one person dedicated to chasing God, I learned how to run. We challenged the status quo in our lives, in our jobs, in our church. She was born to push. She hadn't grown up in Christianity—her family was Muslim—so there weren't years of traditions to uphold, only endless energy to grow closer to God. She complemented my strengths and wasn't willing to accommodate any weakness she felt God was calling me to address. And somehow, in that sacred time in the car each week, we experienced synergy. More together than we could apart.

Apparently, I was wrong about that Venn diagram. If you look closely, the circles were touching at one single, solitary point. The absolute only thing we had in common was Jesus. And he was more than enough.

When she moved away, I was afraid I wouldn't find a friend like that again. And it's true—she was irreplaceable. But now I knew how to be a better friend. And we're designed to play on a team.

God has graciously brought others into my life since then. And I wouldn't be who I am now without the amazing, loving care of my friends. The women in my life are game changers. Frequently, the faces within the circle change. But the love in the center does not. These women know me. Not a fake version of myself wearing the social emotional equivalent of Spanx, but *me*. My Romans Seven Self's sinful holdouts, and the ezer-warrior who fights for her birthright in the kingdom.

God even sent me a beautiful soul with whom I felt safe enough to share my warrior journals. She listened to me explain why I talked to Peter like he could hear me, and instead of finding it weird, she found it awesome. One time we found a boat on the side of the road—a *boat*—and we shoved it into the minivan and hauled it into my house. Then we read all the passages of Jesus and the disciples out on the sea. While in that boat. In my house. Because God isn't opposed to crazy, wild, and fun. He's the author of it.

These women are the church. They are my community. And they make me laugh until I run for a restroom. I recently climbed into my car to drive home after having been with these women for a weekend. And I wept. So hard that I had to pull over and use Burger King napkins for tissues. I wondered why I was crying.

And then I realized this was joy in its purest form. Real and unhindered by circumstance. Tethered to the heart. We have never seen God, but if we love one another, God lives in us and his love is made complete in us. Every once in a while, the team gets a taste of heaven. A glimpse of the kingdom. In the completeness of God's love, there's no lack and no want. The sponge is full—full of God, full of love.

And the sponge so full, so satisfied, can only cry out with tears of joy.

CHAPTER 13

The End of the Beginning

If, when stung by slander or ill-nature, we wax proud and swell with anger, it is a proof that our gentleness and humility are unreal, and mere artificial show.

—Francis de Sales, *Introduction to the Devout Life*

ONCE UPON A TIME, I THOUGHT GOD WANTED ME TO WRITE A book to change the world. Turns out he wanted me to write a book to change me. Arguably the bigger miracle.

It's been years now since I began this wild, free-range journey of faith and Scripture. I would love to tell you that I'm free from people pleasing and never stress about getting dressed. I yearn to report that aging is a blessing and I'm looking forward to the seasons to come. It would be a fabulous ending to say I'm blissfully fulfilled because I finally know who I am and whom I serve. But that's just not true.

And truth telling seems to be my one spiritual gift.

As my journey rolled along, I spent significant energy attempting to fix the system that had produced me—a Good Christian with no real faith. I stomped into my house of worship and generously shared how we needed to shake things up. Stop doing the same old stuff. Get out of our ruts. I wrote and led Bible studies with radical fervor. I eliminated tables that were too large and forced people to cram around TV trays. I hauled a refrigerator door into the sanctuary so we could sit in God's kitchen. I took a bunch of women into a cemetery at night so we could ask the gravestones about our priorities.

What a weirdo.

I thought that God called me to break out of the staleness of a culture that tolerated unsalty salt. Perhaps I was supposed to bring the breath of fresh air I had found into the beige complacency of modern, Western belief. And while I was certainly behaving like a warrior, I had slightly missed the embodiment of ezer. And trajectory is everything when it comes to moving forward.

I probably owe a blanket apology to 90 percent of the people who knew me in my thirties. Here it is. Attention, long-suffering servants who were just trying to make the taco salad. Listen up, dear ones who planned craft nights for middle-aged white women. I hope you can hear me from your post in the nursery or from the church basement as you reorganize the flannelgraph figures. There was so much I didn't know. Apparently, Jesus is okay with Bunco. And if you host a ladies' talk about winter versus summer colors, God can be glorified in the process. He's just that big.

For a long while, I thought the process of *doing church* was suspect. Anything that had caused confusion or pain for me—such as the term *Quiet Time*—must be rejected. My version of rebranding looked a lot like Sherman's visit to the South. But time is a good mediator, and as the years passed I discovered that mostly I was rebranding the human need to be comforted without surrendering to the Comforter. That the Bible studies and events and programs were just Bible studies, events, and programs.

And so I wondered—what, then, was the answer?

Why wasn't our saltiness making more of a difference? Why weren't we more effective at relieving the suffering that seeped deeper into our communities with every passing year? I was saddened by our collective lack of progress. I witnessed the metamorphosis of deeply committed servants who developed a jaded form of detachment, expecting little to nothing.

As I grew older and became removed from the wave of generational grooviness, my new perspective yielded alarming observations. The church appeared to be relying upon the young to come in with energy and vision that was much more based in the naïveté of youth than we might like to admit. I was confused. I thought righteousness was life sustaining. Discipleship pulled generations together, weaving a deep fellowship regardless of worldly status. But now older—and, perhaps, wiser—I could see that all my attempts to change church had yielded mostly a crop of hurt feelings.

Because it wasn't the system that needed reformation. It is, and has always been, the Good Christian.

Outside the church I encountered more and more people convinced of the bleakness of postmodern thinking—there is no truth, only relative moral codes. These people believe being a good-ish person and living a good-ish life are all we can or should aspire toward. And within this worldview, a dissenting voice was most often characterized as bigoted and uneducated.

But inside the church, I experienced much of the same self-absorbed intolerance—an us-versus-them mentality that left me feeling tired.

As my energy ebbed and flowed, I wondered how the ezer sustained her fervor. How do we carry on with the minutiae of life while developing an all-consuming passion for God? The process of opening our minds and hearts to God involves startling revelations into the depravity of our own character. It's quite sobering to know even our most noteworthy résumé points are equivalent to used sanitary napkins. Thank you, Isaiah. With continued growth, my view widened out from a personal level to become increasingly aware of how humanity has rejected—and continues to reject—our Servant King. Like many before me, as I gained insight into this collective snubbing of our heroic God, I was at risk of becoming righteously indignant on his behalf.

So the fire in my bones, initially burning with consistent force, was threatened by discouragement and by my own slow progress as well as humanity's indifference to God's mercy and forceful rejection of his grace.

The primary roadblock in my progress as a warrior was that I needed something to fight. It felt right to find fault in the system, and then replace the old program with something new and exciting. The big surprise for me came when I saw the cycle repeat itself as the younger church members fought for their idea of *authentic* by abandoning so many of the great ideas we had previously established. This incredibly serpentine experience yields a simple truth: Deeper faith doesn't come from a program, nor does it come from a lack of programs. Discipleship is an intensely personal journey. No matter how hard we as herd animals try to create a formula or recipe, human hearts will not be easily mortified. Just as we can't *believe* for another person, we can't *grow* for another person.

No amount of programming will make something dead grow. It's truly hard to be this brilliant, but please stick with me. The Bible is full of agricultural metaphors constantly driving home the notion that there's no such thing as Googling deeper faith. It's a slow and laborious task to cultivate a seed as it grows.

So as I stumbled forward in my ezer training, I learned that what appeared to be obstacles, roadblocks, and static was actually—drum roll, please—my life. The only fight to consistently engage in was within. A daily taking up of the cross. My Romans Seven Self was a vast mission field.

This is the truth that every hero who lives to old age will tell you: There's no greater enemy than Romans Seven. But don't despair. Becoming a slave to righteousness will gradually yield something more amazing than any single victory. It will yield a heart that beats for Jesus alone. And then freedom is limitless.

Just ask Daniel.

Dan. Dan the Man. You know the guy. The dude who was thrown into a lion's den by his conniving enemies. Then God saved him, and in a very satisfying moment of justice, Dan's enemies were tossed into the den themselves. I was familiar with Daniel's big moment. Lions, blood, victory. But Dan's story is so much more complicated, in the same way that our lives are complicated. Although black and white do exist, we all live, work, and die in a world of gray.

Daniel is only a teenager—a noble youth—when his flailing kingdom is ransacked by Nebuchadnezzar. Described as handsome and young, Daniel is carried off to slavery in Babylon. His family is never mentioned, but everybody knows how Nebuchadnezzar solves his problems—murder. This is where I find Daniel. This is where I can see a tiny seed in the earth.

A shattered life. No future, no plan, and yet still alive.

Like all dictators, Nebuchadnezzar understands the easiest way to conquer a culture is to demoralize it. Spare the young. Take the best and the brightest and strip them of their former identity, brainwashing them into model citizens of the new regime. Then place these super converts in authority over their own countrymen. No full-blown rebellious thoughts can develop if they're smothered in their infancy deep within the broken heart.

Daniel is ripped from the tether of his home, his parents' hopes and dreams, and the comforts of his religious practices. Convention is gone, along with morality and justice. Now there's only survival, proving once again there are worse fates than dying young.

In this free-falling existence—long before his enemies know his name—Daniel the warrior is born. The text says Daniel set his heart. He resolved. In the midst of incomprehensible loss, Daniel chooses God. And this is the essence of warrior life. Choosing God because he is God, because it is the only reasonable action.

Daniel and his friends landed in Babylon and were basically offered all the enticements of Vegas. The whole point of retraining was to give the young bucks everything they'd never had. "Boys, we have the answer to your every question. We're here to fulfill your every desire. You're one of us now."

In resisting the temptation to conform, how did they also resist the temptation to become angry?

Many evenings as I read Daniel's story, I would slip into the darkness of ancient Babylon in search of answers.

Finding Daniel in a circle of friends, I listen closely to the debate. I see many hardened faces in the group. Sullen and belligerent, they hate the men holding them captive.

"We will never be Babylonian. Should we not fight? Should we not spew curses upon our captors?"

In the circle I feel the strong pull of vengeance. Anger is a byproduct of powerlessness.

"They've killed our families and taken us as prisoners to a foreign land. They've defiled our temple and stolen our sacred artifacts. And now they wish to reform us—to strip us of our names, our culture, our heritage. Let's take the meat and wine they give us and throw it in their faces. Let them kill us, and we'll die a righteous death!"

Perhaps death would've been easier. But Daniel's heart was set. He wouldn't buy what the Babylonians were selling, but he wouldn't give in to hatred either.

Unwilling to break God's law by eating forbidden foods, he politely asks his captors if he might consume only vegetables and water. He negotiates with the enemy. Daniel won't compromise God's commands. But he compromises everything else. He remains faithful to God but also obedient to his captors. Throughout his life, we see this guy consistently and generously serving those who seek to oppress him.

Daniel's meekness is hard to understand. How was he uncompromising in his faith while still helping the enemy? I wonder if his behavior seriously angered the devoted refugees stranded in Babylon. Was he labeled a sellout who compromised his faith in lieu of the king's favor? Daniel's kindness toward those who had violently destroyed his homeland and desecrated God's temple was incomprehensible. And we know that Daniel's demeanor, while earning him favor with a series of regimes, only solidifies his standing as an outsider and kindles murderous jealousy among many people of power and influence.

This great guy really had no way to win.

That's what stumped me. And that's why I stayed in Babylon, reading his story over and over. The man prayed three times every day for his homeland, his people, and his freedom, only to die after seventy some odd years as a slave. It seemed obvious that Daniel's life was mostly one of loss.

So I go back to the water and the vegetables. I stand with the group of friends and wonder if I can follow Daniel when following him feels like giving in. Not that long ago I rebelled at the very thought of living life on God's terms, bound by circumstances that were unwanted or unchosen. I believed that praising God in the midst of the storm was basically letting God off the hook or failing to hold him responsible for suffering. I demanded that God give an account for his lack of action. And I called it prayer.

But standing in Babylon, my heart begins to focus. Daniel isn't surrendered to Nebuchadnezzar—he is surrendered to God. If God commands that he live as a slave and bless those who hold him captive, then he will live as a slave to the glory of God. He extends kindness and grace that stems from the Giver of all good things. Some of Daniel's friends do, too, even while suspended between their old culture and this new one.

The space between. Now I could see the origin of my perpetually ruffled feathers. God called me to peacefully eat vegetables and drink water much more often than he called me to swing a sword.

The fruit of the spirit is the identifying mark of the ezer. Not her armor, not her weapons. Unless we steadfastly reject the need to claim our rights in the land of Romans Seven, we can't grow. And if we aren't growing, we're probably just rotting.

This is the lesson of Dan the Man. Contentedness.

Despite the ruthless attempts to conform his heart, Daniel knows who he is. He is a child of Yahweh. Because his identity is in God, he can work alongside magicians who worship evil and serve darkness. He can sit at the table with pagans as they eat their unclean food. He can treat the king with respect even as that king kills his kinsmen. He can live inside the machine without being overcome by the mechanisms because he didn't have an agenda of his own. He didn't have a brand to protect or a need for validation. They can call him the Prince of Baal and he'll answer to it, knowing it doesn't change his true identity.

Generic niceness is very anticlimactic. But here in Babylon, I see the long game of the warrior. We have only God. We can refuse to serve ourselves while also refusing to become bitter.

This is how Daniel lives a black-and-white life in a world of gray. With God's power, his posture is one of sacrifice. He is respectful, kind, and unassuming. He's the smartest guy in the room yet has no problem making the coffee. Because God's power is sustaining him, he's able to resist the perverse comfort that hatred offers.

I penned long questions in my journals, asking God, "How do I do this? How do I hold the line without drawing lines? How can I be impenetrable as iron but not defensive? How should I promote inclusivity while remaining set apart? How can I pray for victory while living in apparent defeat?"

Slowly, my little seed grew. I learned to be wary of any subculture, Christian or otherwise. Turns out there can be unseen adversaries within a subculture and unseen friends outside it.

Every night, scribbling in the journals, he led me one painstaking step at a time. Whenever I felt pressure to draw a line, I gave the line to God. When I felt pressure to defend myself, I gave my defense to God. When I wanted to conform in order to buy a bit of comfort, I gave my comfort—or lack of it—to God. It felt like a slow death, sort of like pulling off my own fingernails. But it was also a slow birth, like a sunrise. This is why I could feel both incredibly defeated *and* relentlessly optimistic.

On really hard days, I asked myself two questions: "What are you trying to protect?" and "What aren't you willing to give?" And it was usually the same answer to both questions—myself. The longer and farther I walked with God, the more I came to accept how often my first, second, and third thoughts were utterly wrong, even as I was trying to do right. Most often, when I felt like rushing to arms, I was to open my arms. And sometimes when I felt comfortable or safe, I was actually in danger and should run for the hills. I learned to question my initial instincts and began developing dependence on the still, small voice in my soul. It was completely disorienting. More and more, Jesus became the only point of reference that was safe to follow.

My dad was fond of saying, "The lions couldn't eat Daniel 'cause he was nothing but backbone." As I lived inside Daniel's world, I discovered his discipline was matched only by his grace. He refuses to bow but also refuses to be angry about it. I discovered that severe discipline, ruthless suffering, and massive injustice had produced—wait for it—a nice guy. And contrary to every superhero narrative, the nice guy ends up saving the kingdom. Toward the end of Daniel's life, a new regime frees the captives and allows them to return to Jerusalem, even underwriting the temple's rebuild. But Daniel's name isn't mentioned in the list of returning exiles. Perhaps he was too old to travel, or maybe there was still work for him in Babylon. But beyond a shadow of doubt, Daniel prayed fiercely for justice—while kindly serving his fellow man—until he breathed his last.

Jesus, the ultimate nice guy, offers salvation to us all. Not by waging a war or by throwing out the old ways in favor of the new or by discarding the broken. He saved us by sacrificing himself. In doing this he finished the war, fulfilled the old ways, and redeemed the broken. He shattered the status quo and inverted the value structure. The poor are made rich. The weak are made strong. And this middle-aged white woman with marginal ability and poor fashion choices is free to sing like a rock star at the stoplight. Because that sunrise outside my windshield was made for me. Blazing pinks, orange, and purple splashed across the sky by a Creator who values me more than all the jewels of Egypt. How could anything beat that?

Living in response to the sacrifice of Jesus—that is the life of the ezer. Quiet and loud. Broken and whole. Listening and speaking. Learning to repent—a lot—and learning to laugh a lot too. I now know what prayer is. And there is really no other way to grow.

It's impossible to explain the color turquoise to someone who can't see. The only hope is to gain sight and see it for themselves. My journey in Slaveworld, awesome and breathtaking as it was and still is, is simply my journey. The only way forward for *you* is your own journey.

Since I went rogue in the hospital parking lot years ago and destroyed my pretty little mug, I haven't accomplished much to be lauded by my culture, my profession, or even my church. But inside, the ezer stands tall. My Romans Seven Self shrinks each day as Romans Eight spreads further across my realm. I'm less fearful of aging or growing irrelevant in my culture. I'm less concerned with the opinions of others. I'm freer to love with my whole heart because I am fully loved. And somewhere along the line, a strange feeling invaded. At first I couldn't identify it.

Recently, I stood in my neighbor's driveway, wearing a giant chicken costume and holding a bunch of balloons, waiting for her to come out to warm up her car. It was her birthday. I looked up into the sky and witnessed the sun pulling free from the horizon. Into my heart came this strange feeling again. It felt sort of like hope and sort of like joy. It felt like strength that had nothing to prove. I watched the balloons bounce against the blue sky. And the ezer knew.

I was content.

Notes

Order Information

REDEMPTION
PRESS

To order additional copies of this book, please visit
www.redemption-press.com.
Also available at Christian bookstores and Barnes and Noble.

CPSIA information can be obtained
at www.ICGtesting.com
Printed in the USA
BVHW030522090223
658196BV00003BB/194

9 781646 456055